THE HONORABLE REV DR KWAME O ABAYOMI

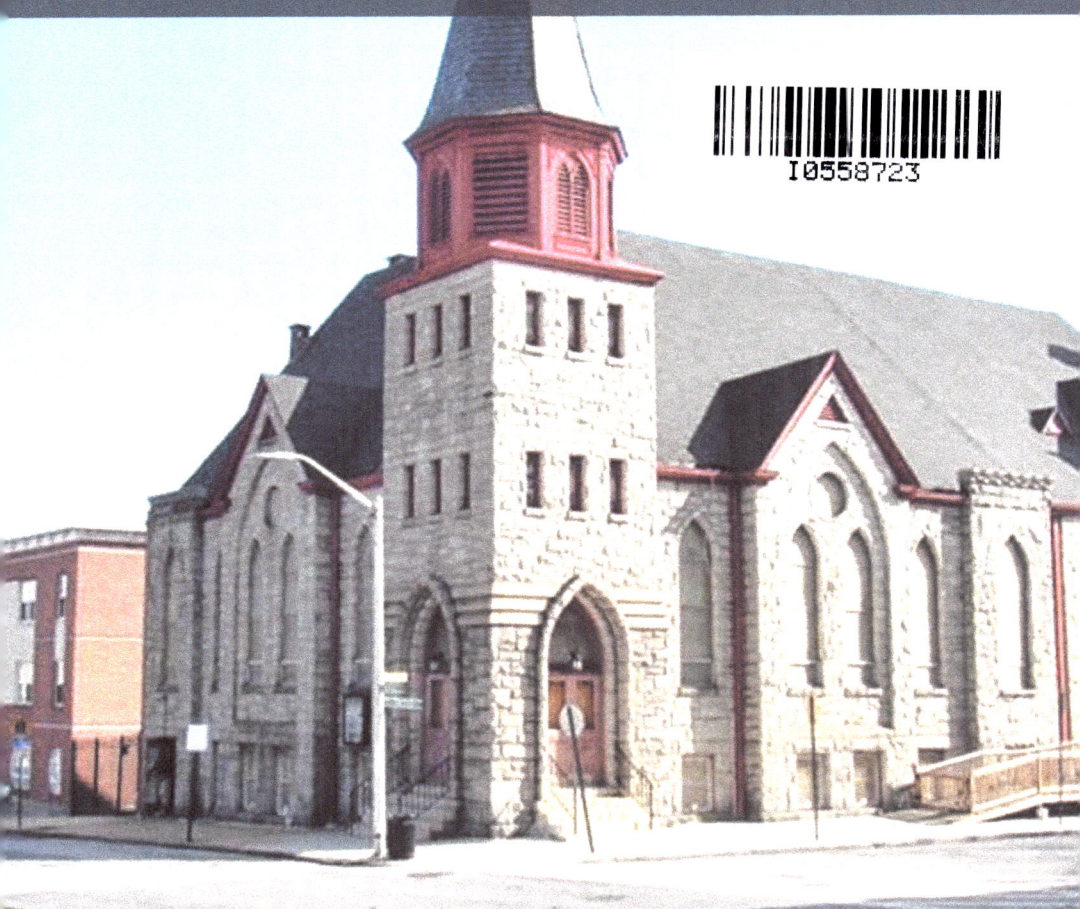

A VOICE IN THE WILDERNESS:

SERMONS AND HOMILIES FOR URBAN MINISTRY

The African-American Creed

A VOICE
IN THE
WILDERNESS

A VOICE IN THE WILDERNESS

SERMONS AND HOMILIES FOR URBAN MINISTRY

with

The African-American Creed

by

The Honorable Reverend
Doctor Kwame O. Abayomi

Volume 1

Foreword by
The Honorable Bishop C. Anthony Muse

Primix Publishing
11620 Wilshire Blvd
Suite 900, West Wilshire Center, Los Angeles, CA, 90025
www.primixpublishing.com
Phone: 1-800-538-5788

Published by Primix Publishing: 03/06/2024

ISBN: 979-8-89194-092-5(sc)
ISBN: 979-8-89194-093-2(e)

Library of Congress Control Number: 2024901268

PRIMIX
PUBLISHING
THE WRITE CHOICE

Foreword

--Some of us have found this calling to speak...
a vocation of agony; but we must speak.
Rev. Dr. Martin Luther King, Jr.

I am ready to preach...
Apostle Paul

I am elated to offer a word on behalf of *A Voice In the Wilderness: Sermons and Homilies for Urban Ministry*, this inspiring collection of proclamations from my colleague and long-time friend, Rev. Dr. Kwame Abayomi. Volume I presents 18 messages from his 25-year career of pastoral ministry that fully elucidate his skill at crafting critical, inclusive, and progressive messages that address the vicissitudes of urban life and living.

Whether his message is evangelistic, doctrinal, or inspirational the anointing of his preaching is crystal clear. Throughout these missives, he succeeds at interweaving an unapologetic interpretation of Black Theology which calls the reader to re-think many conservative doctrines, outdated traditions, and contemporary misunderstandings of Christianity. Another aspect of his preaching style is the use of autobiographical anecdotes. It helps him to more closely identify with his audience whether preaching a traditional Sunday morning worship or a Jazz Vesper Service. An old adage of the Black Church says: "learnin (scholarship) and burnin' (the Holy Ghost) can dwell under the same roof on friendly terms." He eloquently achieves that here.

As you peruse these pages, I encourage you to fasten your spiritual seat-belt, and hold on to your Bible as this servant of God preaches the Word of God for a time such as this.

The Honorable Bishop C. Anthony Muse

(The Honorable Bishop C. Anthony Muse is the founder, Presiding Prelate, and Senior Pastor of Ark of Safety Christian Church and World-Wide Denomination, headquartered in Upper Marlboro, MD. He is the 1st African-American Minister to be elected a State Senator in MD, serving the 26th Legislative District. In 2012, Bishop Muse made history when he became the 1st African-American Minister to candidate for the U. S. Senate from Maryland.)

Dedication

Audrey Estelle (Williams) Powers   1920 -1982

This book is dedicated to my mother and step-father, Audrey (Williams) and Clarence J. Powers; my grandmother, Clara (Williams) Johnson; my grandfather, Rev. "Singing" Jimmy Williams; my great-grandmother, Susie Reeder Duff; my great-uncles, Rev. Dr. Lloyd N. Young, and Rev. Robert Baddy; my pastor, Rev. Robert Owen Johnson; my son, Norman (Tony) Handy, Jr., my partner and editorial consultant, Dr. Shirley Mary Childress; and the officers and members of Unity United Methodist Church in Baltimore, MD.

These souls—and many others—have helped forge the links in my spiritual chain. Our connectedness to each other and to God have sustained me on this pilgrimage and inspired these words. May these sermons and homilies inform and challenge the souls of all who read them.

Ashai, Alleluia, Amen!

The Honorable Reverend Doctor Kwame O. Abayomi

Introduction

The term "Urban Ministry" was first coined for usage by large—predominately White—denominations to describe the work their churches performed in cities. Later, the term morphed into describing ministry specifically provided to the poor, disenfranchised, homeless, and unemployed (the socially marginalized) of the city. It has, since, evolved to mean the work Christians and churches perform for the later; and how those souls and issues are addressed systemically and individually within the confines of declining human and financial resources.

The sermons proffered here represent my efforts to "tell the story", while serving as the Senior Minister of Unity United Methodist Church (UMC) in Baltimore, MD, from 1989 until my retirement in 2006.

They are didactic by design, inspirational by intent, and almost all were delivered in the ambiance of what my Homiletic Professor, Dr. Evans Crawford described in his treatise, *The Hum of Black Worship*/1: they were punctuated with ecclesiastical epitaphs and exclamations, such as, "Help him preach, Holy Ghost", or "Tell the story, Pastor", or "I hear you, Preacher!"

This reprise of almost 25 years of my preaching efforts is part of a larger urban ministry that was both conceived and implemented through the tireless efforts of the officers and members of Unity United Methodist Church. In May, 1989, I received a Doctor of Ministry (D. Min.) Degree, with a major in Church Administration from Howard University School of Divinity in Washington, DC. I was convinced by theorem and praxis (I had pastored four (4) churches before I graduated) the implementation of effective and efficacious urban ministry required the organizing of money or people. As was the case with most urban congregations, Unity's abundance lay in the latter, so we set about galvanizing our resources.

Our theory and sphere of ministry hinged on the understanding that Unity's response to the challenge of urban ministry, must be holistic in form—it must address body, mind, and soul.

We were convicted by the words of Dr. Martin Luther King, Jr., that: "any religion (or church) that professes to be concerned with the souls of men, and is not concerned with the slums that damn them, the economic conditions that strangle them, and the social conditions that cripple them is a dry-as-dust religion./2"

The Setting

Harlem Park, in Baltimore, MD was the first neighborhood in the United States to be designated as an "Urban Renewal Community." Granted in the 1950's under President Dwight David Eisenhower, it was the first community in the nation to receive Federal re-development funds to address the social and environmental malaise (high crime, unemployment, and drop-out rates, etc.)) within it's borders.

However, by the year of my appointment to Unity UMC, it was—by every social indice—one of the most socially devastated communities in the city.

Baltimore had been designated "the city that bleeds" by the national press, because it had one of the highest murder rates in the nation. Between 1990-1999, there were more than 300 murders per year!

The Western District Police Station located in the adjacent community of Sandtown-Winchester had been dubbed the "wild, wild, west" because of the level of crime and violence extant. (From 2001-2003, the first murders committed in the city occurred in Harlem Park and Sandtown-Winchester.) /3

Harlem Park Middle School was ranked 27th out of 28 for scholastics' and truancy. There were 13 liquor stores within its 12-block area, and during the "crack-drug epidemic," many of these stores were the site of an "open-air drug market." Of the more than 2500 addresses there, 720 were vacant and/or abandoned. According to the 1990 Census Report, the teen pregnancy, illiteracy, incarceration, and drop-out rates were some of the highest in the city. While it's household income, literacy, and high-school matriculation rates were some of the lowest/4.

Urban Ministry: Its Design and Development

Some of Unity's many ministries were designed and conceived to confront issues on a systemic-basis. This involved creating several 501(c)3 organizations. Under the leadership of

Minister Michael P. Carter, Wholistic Counseling, Inc. became certified by the Maryland Department of Health & Mental Hygiene (DHMH) to provide out-patient drug treatment. Through it, the church birthed the first HIV/AIDS Ministry in Baltimore. In 1992, it's coordinators Paul Kelly and David Horner were interviewed on ABC's, "Nightline," by host Ted Koppel. Wholistic Counseling, also, convened a Symposium on HIV/AIDS at Howard University Divinity School in 1989. It was attended by 270 religious and faith leaders from the District of Columbia, Maryland, and Virginia (DMV). (I still recall the sermon preached by the Honorable Reverend Doctor Susan Johnson-Cook, "An Issue of Blood.")

UMOJA Housing Corporation (UHC) was formed to address the blight of decent and affordable housing in Harlem Park and Baltimore City. In 2004, UHC completed an $11.2-million dollar, 74-unit, low-income apartment complex.

Still another ministry, UMOJA Head Start Academy began operation in May, 1995, under the leadership of Mrs. Helen Spence. Under the helm of Minister Millie B. Rice, the Academy has become the third largest in the city, operating three (3) sites, and providing educational and child-care services for more than 250 families.

Under the rubric of addressing issues on an individual basis, over 53 separate ministries were birthed in that cauldron of faith and works, including: a soup kitchen, clothes-closet, Saturday School, Chess Club, as well as ministries of African Dance & Drumming, Modern Dance, Book Club, SHARE, Senior, Bereavement and Sick & Shut-In.

Finally, a word about the African-American Creed. When I was ordained an Elder in 1982, I raised the question, "why was there no A/A Creed in our hymnal?" Other groups (Native American, Korean) had theirs. There was even a Canadian Creed; but, none for African-Americans. So, I composed one. After several, unsuccessful submissions to hymnal committees for inclusion in their respective and prospective worship resources, I have published it here for your use and edification.

Ashai, Alleluia, Amen

The Honorable Reverend Doctor Kwame O. Abayomi

About The Author

The Honorable Reverend Doctor Kwame Osayaba Abayomi

Dr. Abayomi (AKA Norman Anthony Handy, Sr.) is the great-grandson of formerly enslaved persons, and a native of Washington, D. C. He is a graduate of Fairmont Heights High School, University of the District of Columbia, Wesley Theological Seminary, and Howard University Divinity School where he received his Doctor of Ministry Degree (D. Min.) in 1989.

He pastored churches in Virginia and Maryland, and was the Senior Minister of Unity United Methodist Church in Baltimore, MD for 18 years until his retirement in 2006. He served as an Adjunct Professor teaching Urban & Community Ministry in the Doctoral-Degree Program at United Theological Seminary in Dayton, OH. He also taught Political Science at the undergraduate and master-degree levels at Sojourner-Douglass College in Baltimore, MD.

Dr. Abayomi founded and served as CEO of several 501(c)3, non-profit organizations:
*UMOJA Housing Corporation—in 2004 successfully constructed a 74-unit, low-income apartment complex at a cost of $11.2-million dollars
*UMOJA Head Start Academy—the third largest program in Baltimore City operating in three sites and serving over 250 families.
*Wholistic Counseling Inc—a drug and alcohol treatment pro-

gram certified by the Maryland Department of Health & Mental Hygiene (DHMH) to provide out-patient treatment.

He also served as President of the Black United Methodist Preachers (BUMP) for all African-American churches from Maryland to Maine, and as Vice-President of the Interdenominational Ministerial Alliance (IMA) of Baltimore.

He is the recipient of numerous academic scholarships, fellowships, and awards. He received a Crusade, a Maryland State Senatorial Scholarship; and, a PEW Foundation Fellowship while matriculating in undergraduate and graduate schools. In 1994, "The City Paper" honored him as "Best of Baltimore." In 1999, he was chosen as "Maryland's Most Beautiful Person" by Governor William Donald Schaefer; and, in 2001 the Baltimore Urban League awarded him the prestigious "Whitney Young, Jr. Award" for Community Service. In 2000, Dr. Abayomi became the first clergy in the nation to receive a W. K. Kellogg Foundation Sabbatical Grant to study in Africa.

In March, 1995 he became the first clergy elected to serve on the City Council of Baltimore. As a councilman, Dr Abayomi chaired several standing committees, including Public Safety, Housing, and Health. He sponsored enactment of landmark legislation, including: a law to regulate Bounty Hunters in Maryland; a law to extend Voting Rights to ex-offenders in Baltimore City for the first time since Reconstruction; and a law that created a Civilian Review Board (CRB) for the citizens of Baltimore. He retired from elected office in 2004. Since his retirement, Dr. Abayomi has traveled extensively throughout Africa and the Caribbean. In 2008, he made a fact-finding trip to Palestine in the Middle-East. He and his partner, Dr. Shirley Childress reside near Negril, Jamaica, W.I. He continues to travel, write, and speak on issues of reparations for slavery and justice for African people.

African American Creed

I believe in one God, who is Creator and Sustainer of all life.

I believe God is the God of all people, God loves and respects all people, and God's son, Jesus Christ, died to save all people.

I believe our God hates sin, but loves the sinner; that all humanity has the *possibility* and the *ability* to come to the fullness and knowledge of God, through Jesus the Christ.

I believe the future of all humanity is interdependent: if one fails, then all are diminished by that failure; if one succeeds, then all are enhanced by that success.

I believe the history of African-American people is richly entwined in the history of all religions, races, ethnic groups, and continents.

I believe we have come from great distances, still have great distances to go, and we are on our journey; we *shall* be free politically, socially, and economically—just as we are free in Jesus Christ, today!

I believe the church of Jesus Christ is the strength of our life: that our past, present, and future are inextricably bound together with all those called by His name.

Ashai, Alleluia, Amen.

The Honorable Reverend Doctor Kwame O. Abayomi

© April 1, 2008

Table of Contents

SERMONS & HOMILIES

"When Are You Coming Home?"

(This sermon was preached at Unity UMC, September 1995 on the occasion of Homecoming.)

Ezra 1:3; Nehemiah 2:6; Revelation 6:10; Luke 15:10

"When are you coming home?" How many times have you heard that question asked lately? "When are you coming home?" It is a question which gets asked millions of times a day by people in all walks of life. Consider the young man who had become highly successful in New York and was heading a Fortune 500 company. He had hundreds of people on his staff, and immense responsibilities. This young man called his mother and was telling her about his wonderful achievements. She listened as he told about his meetings, of million-dollar budgets, and all the powerful people he knew. Finally, he noticed her quietness, so he asked,"Mother, are you still there?" "Yes," she said, "all that's good, but, son, when are you coming home?"

Beloved, this is a question, the asking of which occurs in all walks of life: if you're late getting home from work, you'll get a call, inquiring, "when are you coming home?"

Even in today's tumultuous and troubled relationships between divorced parents, the children are saying (in their hearts, if not aloud) to the absent parent, "when are you coming home?" People who used to go to Unity; but, who haven't been here in a while will often be asked (when seen by one of us),"when are you coming home?" Many times, the response will be, "I'm working on my degree," or "I'm trying to build up my business, and ain't got time, right now," or "I'm involved in some very important undertakings..." Yet, despite all the things they are involved in, despite all the places they have been, and despite all the places they are planning to go—the question remains, "when are you coming home?" (And, that brings me to my text.)

This Homecoming message considers three questions posed in three separate scriptural circumstances: one in Ezra, one in Nehemiah, and one in Revelation. In Ezra, Israel had been in exile for many years in the country of Babylon. (Babylon was located where Iraq and Iran are today, it's capital was Baghdad!) The mighty temple of Solomon had been destroyed by the Babylonians, and the people of Israel were given permission to go home and renovate their temple.

Ezra's question to Israel was simple, "who amongst you is willing to go up to the city of Jerusalem and completely rebuild the temple of our God?" Many came forth, brought their gifts and talents, made the journey home, and completely renovated their church. They restored it so well, it was a sight to behold and a testament to the greatness of Israel's God.

The second question is in Nehemiah. About 70 years after the temple had been rebuilt, Nehemiah, now a cupbearer in the king's court, asked and received permission from the king to go home and rebuild the walls of the temple. The king asked him one question, "How long will it take you to get home?"; and, "when are you coming back?" He gave no answer; but, (scripture tells us) he was prepared to go home as quickly as he could and work until the job was done.

The third question is found in The Revelation of Jesus Christ to John. The Saints of God, who had been slain and persecuted during the great tribulation were waiting under the altar in this vision. Impatient to receive their reward in glory, the Saints asked, "How long?" How long would it be before the gates of glory swung open for them.

Together, the three questions address our occasion: "who is willing to come home?"; "how long will it take for you to get here?"; and, "how long before we all get home?" I want to propose a forth query for our list: "where is home?"

In the broadest sense of the word, home is where the heart is. In the spiritual realm, home is the place where the flame of faith first began to flicker. It is the place where you first learned the meaning of being "saved," and gave your personal commitment to serve God without hesitation or reservation.

You may climb the prodigious mountains of New Hampshire, or walk the meandering banks of the muddy Mississippi, or bask in the warmth of California beaches; but, "there's no place like home!

Your soul may be lifted on high by the power of the Mormon Tabernacle Choir, or the Florida Mass Choir; but, "there's no place like home."

*You may consort with kings, be greeted by great princes, and feast your eyes upon the Taj Mahal...

*You may visit the pyramids of Egypt, dine in splendor atop the Eiffel Tower...

*Whether you travel to Poland or Peru, to Tokyo or Timbuktu; whether you go to the top of the Himalayas, or to the bottom of the Grand Canyon—there's no place like home!!

The Saints of God who have longed for rest and peace plumbed the meaning of the word when they sang, "I got a new home over in glory, and it's mine, mine, all mine."

The elegance of the rehabilitated temple was a sight to see; but, there remained much work to be done.

Likewise, our church has beautiful and comfortable pews, with air-conditioning and newly painted walls; but there's still much work to be done! So, the cupbearer's query of old is still relevant and calls out to you, today, "when are you coming home?"

Hungry minds gather every Sunday to sit at the feet of our Sunday School Teachers; but, we need more teachers—"when are you coming home?"

Trembling voices in our choir strive (and succeed) with holding up their part of the harmony; but, we need more choristers—"when are you coming home?"

Our young folk are tired of hearing a sermon, they would rather see one; we need more moral models for them to follow—"when are you coming home?"

We have "sick and shut-in" members who yearn for a visit or a call from anyone. We need more saints who believe that when one of us suffers, all of us suffer; who believe we must all share the responsibility of caring, so we can all share the blessing—"when

are you coming home?" Listen:
*our elderly are starved for a moment of attention;
*the homeless in our hoods are crying out for a "crust of bread, and a corner to sleep in...";
*the social conditions of our community require a collective response from the church;
*our babies are having babies, and they are only babies themselves;
*too many of our teenagers are "dead on arrival" (DOA) into adulthood from overdoses of "lead poisoning";
*our schools are failing; "when are you coming home?"

But, let me be a bit more specific: God is saying to someone here, "when are you coming home?"

There is the story of a young man who left home to make his way in the world. His parents were anxious and excited for him, and with their blessing, off he went to the big city. At first, the letters were frequent and cheerful, full of good news and tidbits of his progress. Soon, they became less and less frequent, 'till finally they stopped all together. Anxious and worried with no word from their son, there was but one thing to do—the father carried an old picture of his son, and off to the city he went to find him.

Upon the father's arrival at his son's last known address, the landlord informed the dear man his son had not lived there in some months. He did know, however, of a club where he had been seen recently.

Bolstered with this news the father visited the establishment, and made inquiry as to his son's whereabouts. Sadly the proprietor informed the father that his son had frequented there; but, had not been seen in some weeks. So, the father—in one desperate act of love—took out that picture, wrote a note on a piece of paper, and (with the owner's permission) placed his "wanted" poster in a conspicuous place behind the bar. The note under the photo read, "Daddy loves you, when are you coming home?"

Oops, there it is! Beloved, we were like that son: prodigal, lost in the wilderness and no word from us went up to our Father's house, either. So, with no word from us, no knowledge of our whereabouts; there was but one thing for our Father to do—he sent his only begotten son Jesus Christ to look for us:
*He came down through 42 generations looking for us;

*He came to Bethlehem looking; but, we weren't there;
*He came to Jerusalem looking for us; but, we weren't there;
*He came to Sychar, to Jacob's well, to Nazareth, and went as far as Bethany; but, we weren't there, either.

Finally, your Lord and my Savior went all the way to Calvary, got him an ol' rugged cross, mounted it, stretched out his hands, and exclaimed to each and every one of us, "DADDY LOVES YOU, WHEN ARE YOU COMING HOME?"

(THE DOOR OF THE CHURCH IS OPEN...)

"Wake Up, Everybody"

(This sermon was preached at Christ UMC in Aquasco, MD on July 6, 1986 for Revival. The title is borrowed from a group of Secular Prophets, known as Harold Melvin and The Blue Notes.)

Mark 14: 32-42

It is incumbent upon us to realize whenever we look at the life of Jesus Christ, we see in his life an example of all those supernal moments that come to us in our human experience. That is we see in the life of Jesus all of the important times and stages of living that impact you and me. *For instance, in the life of Jesus, we see—pristeenly clear—the moment which comes to every family when a child is born.* It was Jesus:

*who left the precincts of glory and through an act of incarnation was born to a teen-aged mother;

*whose earthly father was an unemployed carpenter—looking for work;

*who came down through 40-plus-two generations; and was delivered in a barn—with only a few shepherds as Godparents..

The scriptures tell us God, himself, got so excited about His "only begotten son's" birth, He had the angels hold a midnight choir rehearsal over a stable in Bethlehem, and sing:

"Joy to the world, the Lord has come.

Let earth receive her King..."

Yes, we see in the life of Jesus, examples of those supernal moments that come in all of our lives! *We see, for instance, the moment that comes when one discovers who they are and whose they are!* It is a problem for a lot of young people, today—they don't know who or whose they are! They have one name on their cap, somebody else's name on their jeans, another name on their tennis shoes, and somebody else's name on their sweatshirt!!! (Is it any wonder they don't know who they are?) But, in Christ Jesus, we see the moment that comes when one discovers *who they are, and whose they are!*

Joseph and Mary had carried Jesus to Jerusalem for the

annual pilgrimage. While they were making oblation to their God, the 12-year old child got lost—or so they thought!! They looked everywhere for him—like any good parents would! And, when they found him, they were amazed at his response to their inquiry as to his recent whereabouts, when he said, "didn't you know that I must be about my Father's business...?"

Again, we see wrapped up in the life of Jesus, a supernal moment, a case-study, a primae facie example of every significant phase of life we go through. So, too, we see the moment which comes in every life—*when God takes notice of your work; and blesses you!* John (his second-cousin, Elizabeth's boy) was holding a Baptism service down by the River Jordan. He looked up, saw Jesus walking on the beach, and exclaimed: "Behold, the Lamb of God, that taketh away the sins of the world!" It seems they got involved in a theological debate about who should baptize whom? After they settled it, John dipped Jesus into the water. Suddenly heaven and earth became skewed:

*a dove stopped it's flight long enough to light on the Savior's head; and,

*God, himself, got on heaven's loudspeaker and declared, hey world, down there, "this is my beloved son, in whom I am well pleased."

We also see in Jesus the moment that comes in every life, called Gethsemane! Gethsemane is the moment when the "hoodlums of the heart", and "gangsters of the soul" put you in their cross-hairs:

*despair slaps you in the face;

*treachery stabs you in the back;

*deceit saddles up beside you for a stay; and,

*conniving takes "pop shots" at your life and livelihood.

Gethsemane is the moment which comes in every life when the soul cries out in anguish: "Precious Lord take my hand, and lead your child on home..." (Let me inquire: has anybody here had a Gethsemane Moment in their life?)

Notice, if you please, Jesus doesn't come to His Gethsemane Moment by Himself—no, no! He brings his "ace-boon buddies", Peter, James, and John with him. And, what does he ask them to do?

*He doesn't ask them to take the sword in their side!

*He doesn't ask them to carry his cross for him!

*He doesn't ask them to take the nails in their hands, his crown of thorns on their heads, or the whip on their backs—no, no! All he asked them to do was "watch, for one hour." But, the text says, "He cometh and findeth them sleeping..." Sleeping?? Sleeping!! Beloved, the hermeneutics of this text are pristeenly clear: when it comes to the work of the church, and of Christ, too many disciples—then and now—are sleeping!!! Oh, we contemporary disciples stay awake for the insignificant, the unimportant, and the mundane—the gossip! But, when it comes to the work of preaching, teaching, and living the Gospel, too many of us are asleep! I just dropped by Christ church to tell you: It's time to wake up, everybody!!! (Can I call the roll?)

*When the church is more concerned about "stained glass windows," then it is about "sin stained souls," it's time to wake up, everybody!

*When young people are more concerned about cash, clothes, and cars than they are about Christ in their lives—it's time to wake up, everybody!

*When children know more about the "Prince of Rock", than the "Prince of Peace"—who'll be their rock in a weary land—it's time to wake up, everybody; and,

*When old folk come to their Gethsemane's either snortin' up, shootin' up, or drinkin' up; instead of lookin' up to the hills, from whence all their help cometh—it's time to wake up, everybody!

I just came by to tell you: God—you do know Him don't you?—is looking for a few good men and a few good women, who will stay awake, and say:

> "You just call out my name,
> And you know wherever I am;
> I'll come running to see you, again.
> Winter, Spring, Summer, or Fall—
> All you have to do is call; and,
> I'll be there. You've got a friend."

Do you mind if I share a story about a young man who once was sleeping; but, who woke up? This lad was born to a middle-class family of five. His parents loved him and his two-brothers very much. He attended parochial schools, and had a great high-school career: He was president of his senior class, editor of his class yearbook, vice-president of the student council, and score-keeper for the baseball and basketball teams. Upon graduation, he decided to attend one of the HBCU's, Morgan State College in Baltimore, MD.

Things went well the first year. In his sophomore year, however, he ran into what the accountant's call, "a cash-flow short-age"—he was broke! This meant: no money—no school; no school—no military deferment; no military deferment—greetings from "Uncle Sam." In order to avoid being drafted, he joined the Air Force.

After 18 months, he found himself stationed in Pleiku, South Viet Nam. 13 months later, he returned from the war under the double-grip of "white death!" He was addicted to both heroin and cocaine!

For the next seven (7) years, he lived the life of an addict: often homeless, penniless, and high, until he was arrested, con-victed, and sentenced to five (5) years in the Georgia Correctional System.

While a prisoner this young man "had a cup of coffee with the Lord!" One Sunday, he went to a church service being held in the prison chapel. A former Catholic Priest, David Wilkerson, who wrote, *The Cross and the Switchblade*, was preaching. Though raised in a Catholic home, this young man heard a different mes-sage about God than he was accustomed.

He heard about a forgiving God, not just a punishing one. He heard about a loving God, not just a stern God." Touched to the quick, when the altar-call was given he found himself walking, leaping, and running to give his life to Christ.

After his "cup of coffee with the Lord", he began his mar-velous journey of renewal and recovery:
*He was paroled in 18 months, and re-enrolled in college.
*In 1981, he received his B.A. Degree in Political Science from the University of the District of Columbia;
*Four (4) years later, he graduated from Wesley Theological Sem-inary, with a Masters of Divinity in Pastoral Counseling;
*Then, in 1989, this man—whose first name is Norman; whose middle-name is Anthony; and whose last name is Handy, gradu-

ated Magna Cum Laud from Howard University Divinity School with a Doctor of Ministry Degree in Church Administration; and, beloved, this is my testimony:

"I've seen the lightning flash, I've heard the thunder roll.
I've felt sins' breakers dashing, trying to conquer my soul
But, I heard the voice of my Savior, telling me to fight on; and He promised never to leave me—never to leave me alone!
No, never alone. No, never alone. He promised never to leave me, never to leave me alone."

I stand here to inquire:"Have you had your 'cup of coffee with the Lord?" Don't fool me tonight:
*I'm not asking to know what your momma had.
*I'm not asking to know what your daddy had.
What I want to know is: Do you know Jesus Christ in the pardoning of your sins? That's when you come awake! And, whenever someone who has been sleeping comes awake, they ought to have an attitude of gratitude in their hearts. When God brings you from darkness to His marvelous light, wipes the clouds of doubt, fear, and failure from your mental skies, their ought to be a song of praise and thanksgiving in your heart and on your lips—you ought to say, "thank you!"

It doesn't matter where you come from, or what nationality you are—when God brings you from the valley of the darkest nights to the mountaintop where the sun shines so bright, you had better say, "thank you." If you're from:
*France—you say, "Merci Beaucoup."
*Germany—you say, "Dunker Shain."
*Spain—you say, "Muchas Gracias."
*Portugal—you say, "Obligato."
*Japan—you say, "Dono Oligato."
*Russia—you say, "Sposiba."
*Ghana—you say, "Medasse."
*Kenya—you say, "Asante Sana."

But since I am—who I am—a nappy-headed, Black man from the ghetto streets of Washington, DC, I simply say, "Thank you:"
*Thank you—for waking me this morning.

*Thank you—for starting me on my way.
*Thank you—for putting food on my table, clothes on my back, and shoes on my feet.
*Thank you—for picking me up, turning me around, placing my feet on solid ground.
*Thank you—for saving my soul, and making me whole.
*Thank you, Thank you, Thank you...

(THE DOOR OF THE CHURCH IS OPEN...)

"Get Your 'But' Out of The Way"

(This sermon was preached at Unity UMC, on March 17, 1990, on the occasion of Unity's 61st Anniversary Service.)

II Kings 5:1-10

The setting of this textual comment by the writer of II Kings is one in which the prophetic career of Elisha is being held up for commendable review—this seems to be the purpose of the proceeding, as well as the following accounts in II Kings. While the episode about Naaman appears to be just a brief insertion about Israel's powerful God, and his prophet, Elisha. And what of this episode? What does it say to us? All we want to consider this morning is set forth in "verse one" of this text:
> "Naaman, commander of the army of the King
> of Syria was a great man with his master,
> and in high favor; because by him, the Lord
> had given victory to Syria; he was a mighty
> man of valor; but, he was a leper."

The identification of Naaman is given to us: "Commander of the army of the King of Syria..." It goes on to say, "He was a great man with his master." He had gained an enviable reputation in the precincts of his own concerns. He was presently enjoying high favor, too. In other words, he was not some "has been" commander—no, no! Because of him, the armies of Syria had known victory, and what's more, he had been instrumental in the Lord's service, an agent of the divine for victorious results—no small achievement. His courage was unquestioned. Valour and bravery were his to know.

Yes, this impressive catalog of assets attended this Syrian commander, and he was identified by them:
> "Naaman, the commander of the army of the
> King of Syria; a great man with his master,
> and in high favor; because of him the Lord
> had given victory to Syria; he was a mighty
> man of valor."

All of this is set over against the final phrase of "verse one." This catalog of attributes, this long list of assets, this man's monumental abilities listed in this verse are set over against this final phrase, "But, he was a leper." "But, he was a leper."

Now, textually and grammatically, this conjunction, "but" was contravening (interrupts), not continuative (connects)—which tells much about what follows. For Naaman, it was a word that clouded his past, and casts doubt on his future. All his positive characteristics, all his assets stood to be nullified by reference to one single, perceived liability which was scornfully associated with his physical appearance:
*no matter what he has gained,
*no matter what his reputation,
*no matter what his assets,
*no matter what his abilities,
*no matter how high he stood, he is lowered in the eyes of those who know him by the content of this phrase, "but, he was a leper."

That was Naaman's problem! Not courage! Not ability! Those weren't his problem. His problem was: he was perceived to have a problem! In other words, when folk looked at him, they had a problem! That was his problem! And, let me tell you something else: for most of us, it is still a problem!

For the question that arises most often, about those of us who have been "kissed by the sun" has very little to do with our abilities, or with our capabilities: (listen)
*he's a fine preacher; but,
*he has been able to get more Democratic voters to register for the primary and general election; but,
*he has won more popular votes than any other Democratic candidate, except one; but,
*he organized an effort to bring an American pilot home from Syria, when the U. S. State Department couldn't; but!
See what I mean? Naaman's problem is our problem, too! It's not about whether we are able. It's not about whether we are insightful, courageous, significant, honest, or trustworthy—that's not our problem. The problem is (Should I say it? Dare I tell it?) The problem has nothing to do with the inside of us. It never gets to how we have struggled, or held on to be whatever we are—no,

no! The problem pays no attention to all we've done, or said. It doesn't behold that. For Naaman, it was leprosy behind the "but;" for Jesse Jackson, it was his Blackness!

Oops, There it is! Naaman and Jesse are perceived to have some difficulty because of their physical appearance! That negates all else they would be, or do. This was Naaman's story. It is Jesse's story. And, it is our story, as well. When anyone has their abilities and their capabilities, their aspirations and their inspiration dimmed and/or damned because their appearance is different, that is the height of indignation and insult.

Be assured, beloved, it is important for us to understand what was behind the "but" in Naaman's life. The "but" in his life was there because another leper didn't write the story:
*if another leper had written the story, but wouldn't have been there;
*if another leper had written the story; it would've read, "AND, he's a leper;"
*if another leper had written the story, the perspective of the leper would have changed the grammar of the text;
*if you let those who don't suffer the malady of the condemnation write your story, you will always end-up behind the but. The definition of who you are will be behind the conjunction of contravention. That's why it's dangerous to let someone else tell your story. Black folk have got to write their own story, if it is going to be told properly.

An African proverb says:
"A lion and his cub came to a clearing in the jungle,
 where stood an eight-foot statue of a white hunter
  with his blunderbuss rifle planted on the head of
 a fallen lion. The cub says to his father, "Why do
 all the statues with lions in them, show us down
 and defeated with the white hunter standing over us?"
 The father replied, "As long as the white hunter tells the
 story, the lion will always be on the bottom."

Yet, there are times, there are instances when we tell our own story, and we do the same thing—we put our own but, in the way! Yes, sometimes, we put a "but" in the way of our own story being all that it could be. Let me make it plain:

*"Pastor, we really ought to build a new church; but..."
*"I really love my wife and family; but..."
*"I am planning to put that cigarette down; but..."
*"I really want to help out more in the church; but..."
*"I'm planning to give my life to the Lord; but..."
Yes, sometimes we can put our own "but" in the way.

That's why I say to "Lottie, Dottie, and Everybody" on this 61st Church Anniversary: Get Your But, Out of The Way. (Let me hurry to a close, lest I keep you too long...)

There is something I see as Gospel in this story, and I don't need a commentary or assisting text to see it. (I want to say this to our ministerial candidates, and serious Bible students, too.) You don't always need to search for the meaning of God's word, sometimes the answer is right there in the structure of the writing, itself. One of the beauties of the Bible is: God composed it, and hid the meaning in plain sight.

So, allow me to repeat myself: "there's some Gospel" in this story that gives us hope, despite the negative meaning of the "but" in it. The reason we can hope and believe everything is going to be alright is: look where the "but" is placed in the story!! It's in "verse one!" This is II Kings, Chapter five, "verse one!" Don't you see? The whole story goes down to verse 10, where it reads, "and, he was made clean." In other words, he does get his "but," out of the way!

Beloved, you and I must not allow ourselves to be stopped and stymied by the "verse one" in our lives, either. If you do, you'll never get your "but" out of the way! You cannot reach the conclusions already worked out for you in the doings of the Divine, if you don't get beyond the "verse one" in your life:

Oh, yes, our "verse one" may be rough on us at times; but, don't let it stop you—no, no— 'cause it's just "verse one!"
*Your "verse one" may mean having to grow up poor, having to go to school with newspapers stuffed in your shoes, and patches sewn on the elbows and knees of your clothes; but it's just "verse one."
*Your "verse one" may mean having to watch as other kids get the chances you never got; just because of "who" their parents were— but, it's just "verse one."

*Your "verse one" may be so rough you can't tell night from day, or right from wrong—but, hold on it's just "verse one"
*Sometimes "verse one" means being told you're too dark, you're too light, you're too poor, your hair's too nappy, you're too ugly, you're from the wrong side of the tracks, you're too dumb, you're too young, you're too old, you're not ready, or you're not the right-type... Whatever it may be, IT'S ONLY VERSE ONE!

" I don't care how young you are
or the length of the race you've run,
being Black is like a scar; but,
it's only "verse one". It seems that
for so long, we've been distressed
with aims and hopes undone;
God's not through with us, yet; and
our "buts" only in "verse one."

I like the way the songwriter put it, long ago:
Farther along, we'll know all about it.
Farther along, we'll understand, "why"
Cheer up, my brother, live in the sun-
shine; we'll understand it, oh, by and
by."

(THE DOOR OF THE CHURCH IS OPEN...)

"Anatomy of A Bestseller"

(This sermon was preached at Unity UMC, in September, 1990 on the occasion of Homecoming.)

Jeremiah 29:11-14; II Timothy 3

Today, I want to take a look at the Bible, using as my subject: "Anatomy of a Bestseller." Since the ancient Babylonians and Egyptians first took papyrus leaves, dried them, used a quill instrument to make legible and lasting impressions on their surfaces, then bound these leaves together with wire, humankind has been fascinated with books. It was not until John Gutenberg invented his printing press in 1450 that bookmaking and book buying became affordable to the average citizen.

What makes the Bible so perpetual? What causes this most controversial of texts to remain the number one, best seller of all times? Is it because it teaches all things to all people? It does teach the golden rule, how to get an answer to prayer, how a husband and wife should get along, and how church members should treat their pastor, too.

I suspect it is so timeless because it contains the mind of God, its' doctrines are holy, its' precepts are binding, its' histories are true, its' decisions are immutable, and its' teachings are inscrutable.

You should read it to be wise, believe it to be saved, and practice it to be holy. You should read it slowly, prayerfully, and frequently; for it is a realm of infinity, a paradise of glory, and a river of pleasure.

There are over 915 languages and dialects spoken on this planet, and the Bible is translated into more than 500 of them. If you can't see, if you can't hear, if you can't read there is still no excuse for you not knowing the Bible. First, we have the spoken word for people who can't see. Then, we have the revealed word for people who can't read or hear! If you can't read, see, or hear, God can reveal His word to you. So, no matter your condition, there's no excuse for not knowing what God wants you to do!

In the 17th century, a man named Dequincy divided literature into 2 classes: the literature of knowledge, which consists of books of information, science, and encyclopedias; and the literature of power, which consists of books that sway the spirit. These are books of imagination, prophecy, and poetry; while the supreme book of power is the Bible.

What makes this book so timeless and timely, so everlasting and exciting, so consequential and at the same time so confusing? Let's take an analytical look at the best seller of all times.

What makes this book so profound? It's because: the world is self-centered, while the Bible is God-centered! You ever noticed whenever you see a history book, whether it's about Whites, Blacks, Jews or Gentiles, the book is about what they did? That's alright! But, the Bible talks about what God did, does, and will do. As good and exciting as history is, none of it would have happened without the providential hand of God.

Think about the number of times you and I give credit to God during an hour, a day, a week. We spend most of our time talking about what we, or somebody else has done—whether we like it or not, whether they knew what they were doing or not; or whether we'd ever do it the same way, or not. But, when you pick up the Bible, there's never any doubt about who's behind every scene on its pages! As James Russell Lowell has said: "right forever on the scaffold, wrong forever on the throne; but, behind the dim unknown standeth God keeping watch above his own."

It's not who you know, or what you know! It's whose you are, and what you are that makes a difference in these days and times. In other words, you can't make it because you've got a Bible on your shelf, in your hands, or even in your head—no, no! The Bible in your heart is what makes the difference between professors and possessors. No wonder the songwriter said:

"Without God, I am nothing. Without God,
I would fail. Without God, life would be
rugged, like a ship without a sail."

Another reason the Bible is the #1 best-seller is: it is the center of true intellectual understanding of life. The world is bewildered:

*With all of our advances in education, we are still in a fog.

*With all our books, we are still blind to the truest meaning of life. But, the Bible contains the best of all books in one book:

*The Bible is not a book on science, yet it is a storehouse of scientific knowledge.

*The Bible is not a book on botany, but it gives a beautiful description of the Rose of Sharon, and the Lilly of the Valley.

*The Bible is not a textbook on geology, yet it talks about the Rock of Ages.

*The Bible is not a book on philosophy, yet it says, "the fear of God is the beginning of wisdom."

*The Bible is not a book on mathematics, yet it tells of the most astounding superstructure ever beheld: a city whose longitude, latitude, and altitude have never been surpassed; a city 1500 miles square.

*The Bible is not a book on astronomy, but it speaks of the sun, the moon, and the stars.

*The Bible is not book on sewing, yet it talks about a seamless garment and robes that were washed in the Blood of the Lamb.

*The Bible is not a book on geology and geography, but it tells how geology and geography became skewed when the water rolled up on both sides as the Hebrew children passed through on dry land.

Yes, you should read it to be wise, believe it to be saved, follow it to be right; for it's medicine to heal us, a guide to lead us, a bit to restrain us, a sword to defend us, and salt to season us.

"As the Civil War was being planned by the South, a White admiral was trying to plot and plan the attack on Fort Sumter, SC. He agonized over how to get near enough so his guns could have effect on the formidable fortress. Someone spoke up and said they had a chart of the harbor which appeared to be accurate; but, it was drawn by a "nigger!"

Now, here was one of the most racist men in the South, being told his planned attack might depend on the drawings of a slave. What do you suppose he did? Do you think he laughed out loud at the prospects of such? At first, the admiral did laugh

Sermons and Homilies for Urban Ministry   35

out loud when he saw the rough sketches drawn in chalk, on the back of a rag. He pondered for a minute, called for a dinghy, ordered his Lieutenant to sound the channel according to the chart, and found it to be just as the slave, Robert Smalls had outlined it."

That, too, is the beauty of God's Word: it doesn't matter who wrote what in it, and it doesn't matter the style of their penmanship—no, no! Just try it, and see if it doesn't work. You see, no one ever read the Bible—read it prayerfully—and became a worse person. If you read it every now and then, and tell God, "Lord, help me to understand it better", you'll have to be a better person. If you become a better person, your loved ones will become better people; and if your loved ones become better people, your home will be a better place. If your home becomes better, your neighborhood will be a better place. If your neighborhood becomes a better place, then our city—you see where I'm going with this don't you?

Can I tell you what you'll read?
*The Bible contains five books of law—they are not the same—they are a powerful source of ethics in government.
*There are 17 books of prophecy (five major, and 12 minor) foretelling of things to come.
*We've got four books of the Gospel, written by four Gospel writers, whose job and purpose was to spread the good news that Jesus came to save from the "guttermost to the uttermost" of us.
*We've got one book of modern history—the Book of Acts: it tells of Jesus going up, the Holy Ghost coming down, and the church going out.
*We've got 21 epistles—those are 21 letters sent by the apostles to certain people concerning their condition and conduct; and,
*One book of modern prophecy—the Book of Revelation.
If you read the Bible, you don't have to go all the way to the New Testament to find out about Jesus, either. You can find him in every book of the Bible:
In Genesis, he's a lawgiver.
In Exodus, he's a Passover Lamb.
In Leviticus, he's a high priest.

In Numbers, he's "a pillar of cloud by day, and a pillar of fire by night."
In Deuteronomy, he's a prophet like Moses.
In Joshua, he's "the captain of my salvation."
In Judges, he's our judge and lawgiver.
In Ruth, he's our kinsman and redeemer.
In First and Second Samuel, he's a trusted prophet.
In First & Second Kings, and First & Second Chronicles, he's an ever-reigning king.
In Ezra & Nehemiah, he's a rebuilder of broken down walls.
In Esther, he's an uncle like Laban.
In Job, he's my living redeemer.
In Psalms, he's a shepherd.
In Proverbs & Ecclesiastes, he's our wisdom.
In Song of Solomon, he's our lover.
In Isaiah, he's our Prince of Peace.
In Jeremiah, he's a righteous branch.
In Lamentations, he's a weeping prophet.
In Ezekiel, he's a four-faced lamb.
In Daniel, he's a lion tamer.
In Hosea, he's a forgiving husband.
In Joel, he's a baptizer with Holy Ghost fire.
In Amos, he's a burden bearer.
In Obadiah, he's mighty to save.
In Jonah, he's a missionary.
In Micah, he's a messenger with beautiful feet.
In Nahum, he's a great evangelist.
In Habakkuk, he works like an evangelist.
In Zephaniah, he's our foundation.
In Haggai, he's our restorer.
In Zechariah, he's a fountain opened in the house of David.
In Malachi, he's a son of righteousness.
In Matthew, he's my Messiah.
In Mark, he's a wonder worker.
In Luke, he's the Son of Man.
In John, he's the word become flesh.
In Acts, he's the Holy Ghost.
In Romans, he's salvation.

In First & Second Corinthians, he's love in action.
In Galatians, he's the fruit of the spirit.
In Ephesians, he's the unsearchable riches.
In Philippians, he's a God who will supply all of your needs.
In Colossians, he's the fullness of the God-head.
In First & Second Thessalonians, he's a soon-coming king.
In First & Second Timothy, he's a study guide.
In Titus, he's a faithful pastor.
In Philemon, he's a friend that "sticketh closer than a brother."
In Hebrews, he's a high priest.
In James, he's bridle on a tongue.
In First & Second Peter, he's the chief shepherd.
In John's book, he's love.
In Jude, he's coming with 10,000 saints.
In Revelation, he's "King of Kings and Lord of Lords."

That makes 66 books we ought to read every now and then. In fact, we ought to read it like we do the newspaper. If you like to read the editorial section, you find that in the Bible, where it says, "be not deceived, God is not mocked; whatsoever a man soweth, that shall he also reap."

If you like human interest stories, they are in there too. Do you remember the story of the Widow of Nain, who had lost her son? Jesus stopped by that funeral procession, and raised him from the dead.

If you like to read the entertainment section, it's in the Bible too. You read that whenever King Saul had an evil spirit, David would play on his harp to soothe his king's soul..

If you like the sports section, that's in there too. You remember where Paul said, 'run the race with patience?"

If you like to read the horoscope section, it's in there. When Job declared "man born of woman is but a few days and full of trouble."

If you like to read about the weather, it's in there. Didn't Noah declare, "it's gonna rain, it's gonna rain."?

If you like to read the comic section, it is in there, too. You remember when Samson tied 300 foxes tails together, lit them, and ran them into the Philistines cornfield producing acres of pop-corn—that's funny!

Some folk like the society column, they want to know who's getting married. You remember when Jesus went to the wedding party in Cana?

Some folks like to read the Obituary Section. They want to know who died, and where they are being buried? That's in the Bible too. Don't you remember? They arrested your lord, and my savior, and drove him up Calvary's hill with a cross on his shoulders. They stretched him wide, hung him high, and he died—you know he died, don't you?

Some folk like to know who is going to preach a funeral. Well, the Roman centurion preached Jesus' funeral, when he said, "surely, surely, this man was the son of God."

Somebody always wants to know who was the undertaker? Joseph of Arimethea was Jesus's undertaker, because he begged Pilate for the body.

Everybody likes to read the headlines—sometimes they don't have time to read much else but those. Well:

*If you want to read the headlines in Miami, you need to get a Miami Herald.

*If you want to read the headlines in Los Angeles, you should get a Los Angeles Times; and,

*If you want to read the headlines in Washington, DC, you had better get a Washington Post.

But, these headlines say the same thing in Africa, say the same thing in Germany, say the same thing in Russia, the same thing from Texas to Timbuktu, from Maine to Maryland. What do these headlines say? "HE ROSE!"

I hear somebody saying, "yeah but Harlem Park Preacher, I wasn't there when he rose, and neither were you. How do you know the headlines are true?" I wasn't there, but I was at a prayer meeting in Brandywine, Maryland one Tuesday night, when he arose in my soul.

That's why I sing:

"At the cross, at the cross;
where I first saw the light,
and the burdens of my heart rolled away.
It was there by faith I received my sight, and now I'm
happy all the day.

The good news is He's coming, again! When the trumpet sounds, first the dead in Christ are going to rise; and, those who remain shall be caught up to meet Jesus in the air. But, I had a serious problem. I was reading one day where there were going to be 144,000 who would go with Jesus when he comes. Well, I knew that many people had died before Moses was born. But, I kept on reading until I got to the place where it says, "I looked and saw a number that no man could number."

*That's the number who have been coming up the rough side of the mountain.

*That's the number who had their robes washed in the "Blood of the Lamb."

When he comes, he's going to give me a brand new robe to wear.. He's not gonna call me Norman—that name has been "'buked and scorned." He's gonna give me a brand new name over in glory, and I will have a song the angels cannot sing—because angels haven't been dug up by the gospel plow.

"Oh, I want to see him, look upon his face.
There to tell forever of his saving grace.
On the streets of glory, let me lift my voice,
cares all past, home at last, ever to rejoice..."

(THE DOORS OF THE CHURCH ARE OPEN...)

"God-Filled Women In This Godless Age"

(This sermon was preached at Unity UMC in May, 1992 on the occasion of Women's Day.)

Ruth 2:1-17 (text 2:16)

"To be or not to be, that is the question." These philosophical words from the lips of Shakespeare's Hamlet about the meaning of life have become for us a matter of survival and existence. For at this hour, the African-American community is battling for just that—survival. In a society that has become disgruntled by the contrary winds of desolation and degradation; in a world that is being seared by the burning suns of disease and sickness; in a country, a state, a city that is being bombarded by the blasts of higher unemployment, and continually declining prospects to get a job; more and more people are singing that old Negro spiritual, "sometimes I feel like a motherless child, a long way from home."

The picture is bleak and dreary wherever you turn. There is hardly any "good news" anywhere, at anytime, from anybody. As a result, people are snortin' up, drinkin' up, smokin' up, shootin' up, and givin' up because they can't straightin' up the tangled web of trouble that is tyin' up their future, and chokin' up their past! The sociologist, the criminologist, nor the psychologist can get to the root of the problem, because the problem is at a deeper level than they are thinking or speaking. The problem is at the very core of our spirit. At that level, there is a "sickness unto death" in our society, Godlessness! I know we face drugs and alcoholism, crime and violence, unemployment and the disintegration of the Black family.

I know we do! But, these are mere symptoms of the problem. It will require radical measures to bring about a meaningful solution. It is going to take poise, piety, and perseverance to cut to the quick of our problem—it is going to take God-Filled Women In This Godless Age!

Since Africans were brought to these shores, there has been

a concerted, deliberate, and nearly successful effort to break up, tear up, and mess up the Black family. Starting in slavery when the only way we could marry was to "jump the broom" until today, when the only advertising to which our neighborhoods are exposed are billboards about a malt-liquor that will "jump start" your life— it has been and remains rough on us!

Through all the stuff we endured as a people in this wilderness of America, it was the creative and salvific actions of Black women that got us through. Yes, through their poise, piety, and perseverance, our people made it:
*it was the creativity of Black women who took the leftovers and crumbs from our enslaver's table, and made dining-delicacies out of them;
*it was the compassion of Black women, who gave new meaning to the word "family" by including everyone's children at their table;
*it was the perseverance of Black women, who kept Black men going when the White world tried to shut them down, or hang them up; and,
*it was the piety of Black women that put fire under preachers, gave dignity to our children, and put balm on our wounded hearts and bodies.

That's what our communities need again—women who won't give up; but, who will stand up for God!
*We have enough women who can hold cocktail glasses, we need women who can hold families together.
*We have enough women who are cute, sassy, and fresh; we need women who are patient, long-suffering, and have love.
*We have enough women who can attack and tear-down; we need more who can support and build-up.
We need God-filled Women In This Godless Age!

(That brings me to my text.)
Of all the women in the Bible, who is the most revered and loved? Is it Esther? Is it Mary, or Deborah, the Queen of Sheba, or Anna? The most revered and respected woman in the Bible is Ruth. Yet, have you noticed there is no biographical data about her, except that she was a Moabite (Moabites were people of an ebony hue.) There is no mention of her age, except we know she was old enough to marry and have children. There is no description of her

habits, or her faults, she is not given any salvific duties for her family or her people. The scriptures do tell us she became the grandmother of David, who was King of Israel. Alas, Ruth's claim to fame is found in a few words from the 16th verse of the book named after her, "your God shall be my God..."

It was not Ruth's pedigree, nor her degrees; not her physical looks, nor the style of her hair; the measurements of her body, or what side of town she lived; not the amount of money in her financial portfolio, nor where she went to school—none of these made her the most popular woman in the Old Testament, and perhaps the Bible. What was it? (I'm so glad you asked...) She is known as the most popular woman in Scripture because she had poise, perseverance, and piety.

(Let me scrutinize these three P's a tad closer.)
The reason I say Ruth had poise was because: *she didn't let the curves and circumstances life threw her way, get in her way!* Ruth held her head high, kept right on struggling and striving to make the best of a bad situation. I can imagine when her husband was alive, things went well for her. She no doubt had dreams of children, one day. Every day she worked hard for the success of her home and marriage—to make it the best home Naomi's boy could have.

Let me pause, and raise an interrogative: What makes a house into a home? Is it the gadgets in the kitchen? Is it the sparkling splendor in the bathroom? Is it the luxury of the living room? Is it the beauty of the bedrooms? Custom hung drapes? Wall to wall carpeting? The central air-conditioning, a color TV in every room, having a freezer full of T-bone steaks? Is that what makes a house into a home? No, no—my sisters! The key that unlocks the mystery to a happy home is God, the presence of Jesus Christ, and the joy of the Holy Spirit! If you don't have these three things in the house where you live, then all you have is:
*custom-draped misery,
*fresh-frozen trouble,
*wall-to-wall confusion,
*untelevised-color-catastrophe, and,
*air-conditioned hell!
Ruth understood, with crystal-clear-clarity, the difference between a house and a home. She didn't stand on her background, nor sit

on some ash heap of trouble. She used all her feminine dignity, and all of the power she found in Naomi's God to keep her head up high, and keep on keepin' on, when times got hard.

My sisters, it's what's needed today! You may be well financed, well heeled, and well dressed. You may be well educated, well organized, beautifully polished and articulate. But, if you don't have the love of God in your life and your home, then you'll be what Brother Paul said in First Corinthians 13: "a sounding brass and a tinkling symbol." I like the way the song poet said it:

"The love of God, guides me along my way.

The love of God never lets me stray.

The love of God will always be there for

the love of God, I know, is everywhere."

Ruth had the perseverance and the piety to go where she had not been, and do what she had not done.

How? *Her faith put her in touch with a man who solved her problems!* You know the story: she accepted her mother-in-law's advice, dressed herself with dignity and poise, went into the fields to glean, and—in doing so—met a man, named Boaz who solved all her problems. That's where I must leave you, today!

Our community is full of "no-good men," too few men, slicksters, hustlers, pimps, thieves, flim-flam artists, men who will whisper sweet words in a woman's ear, and leave them high and dry when the morning comes. But, just as Ruth found out:

*there is a man who will "stick closer" than a sister or a brother and love you forever like no other;

*there is one, I know, who will love you so, and honor and vouch-safe your blessed name;

*there is one who will love each of you, just as if he didn't have anybody else to love;

*there is one who's a true friend, like no other.

I heard the songwriter say:

"There's not a friend, like the lowly Jesus;

No not one, no not one. One who can

heal all our souls' diseases—no, not one,

no not one. Jesus knows all about our

troubles, He will guide 'till the day is

through. There's not a friend, like the

lowly Jesus—no not one! No not one.

(You don't mind if I testify, do you?)

It was June, 1950. I remember as if it was yesterday. It was the day my mother and father separated. My momma waited until we finished the school year, then packed up our clothes and belongings, and moved us to live with my Godmother across town. After my two brothers and I unpacked our things, got dinner, had our baths, and were getting ready for bed—all of a sudden, all three of us boys began to cry. Softly, at first; but, then louder and louder until we were at a full scale wail! We didn't know what we were crying about! We didn't know whether it was because we were no longer going to be living with our father; or because we were glad to be free of having to wake up in the middle of the night to hear him beating on our mother! We didn't know what it was; but, there we were ballyhooing and wailing at the top of our lungs. Then, in the doorway, stood my mother—all five feet, two inches of her! She tried to calm us for some time. Finally, all cried out, my older brother spoke up, and said, "Momma, what in the world are we gonna do without Daddy?" My mother looked at us, and through eyes that were certainly stained by this failed marriage, and the prospect of raising three African-American boys in Amerika, and said, "the Lord will make a way, somehow." She didn't tell us "how," she told us "who"—"the Lord will make a way, somehow."

That was over 40 years ago. I didn't understand what she meant when she said it, then; but, when I stood at her graveside some ten years ago, I said, "thank you, Momma!" This woman worked two jobs, so we could attend parochial school, have food on our table, and clothes on our back. She showed us by precept and example, by letting her piety (her belief in God) guide her way and her walk.

Beloved, that is the "meat" in my message, today, the Lord will make a way, somehow:

*for all of you who have been in the storm too long...

*for those who are floundering between every wind and doctrine...

*for all of you who are wondering how you're going to make it...

*for all who are stuck in the past, drowning in the present, and living in abject fear of the future...

I cannot tell you how you're going to make it; but, I can tell you who will get you through whatever it is you're going through: the Lord will make a way, somehow:
*I know who can pick you up when you fall...
*I know who will comfort you when you're all alone...
*I know who will be a friend, when you can't find any...

> (Seems I hear Ruth singing this morning:)
> "Like a ship that's tossed and driven, battered by
> an angry sea;
> When the storms of life are raging, and their fury
> falls on me,
> I wonder what I have done,
> that makes this race
> so hard to run;
> Then I say to my soul, take courage,
> the Lord will make a way somehow."
> (Seems I hear my Momma singing:)
> The Lord will make a way somehow,
> when beneath the cross I bow,
> He will take away each sorrow,
> let Him have your burdens now.
> When the load bears down so heavy,
> the weight is shown upon my brow,
> There's a sweet relief in knowing
> the Lord will make a way somehow."

(THE DOOR OF THE CHURCH IS OPEN...)

"Let's Go Get Stoned"

(This sermon was preached at Unity UMC in June 7, 1992.
The title is borrowed from the Secular Prophet, Ray Charles.)

Acts 2:1-21 (v.15)

This week, I had the honor and privilege of speaking for the Awards Assembly at Harlem Park Middle School. While on my way to the school, I heard something out of the mouths of three young men that caused me to pause along my walk. I had gone but a few steps along the walkway, when I saw them. If they were going to school, they were obviously going to be late.

As I drew closer, I heard one of the youths say to the other two, "yo, ain't you going to school, we only got one more week?" The larger of the other two threw his hand up in the air (as if to ward off the very thought) and with an air of disdain, replied, "naw, I ain't going to no (expletive deleted) school, "let's go get stoned!"

Now, I admit my sensitivities were shocked, and my conscience clamored at the very thought of these boys—none of whom appeared to be over 13—opting for the "highway," instead of the pathway of study and learning. As I pondered my surroundings, and thought about the times we're living in, it occurred to me that while I heard it from these kids, there are a lot of grownups, who by their actions, are saying, "let's go get stoned." Hear this, today: *College graduates are saying it! The class of 1992 faces the bleakest prospects of finding a job in their major, once they finish college. In fact, only graduates finishing a military academy, or a degree in math, natural and health sciences, or education can expect to earn an income above that of their friends who only finish high-school! So, many of this year's class are saying, "let's go get stoned!"

*Parents are saying it! Children are growing up faster than ever. They are staying out later, learning to curse earlier, quitting school sooner, getting pregnant or fathering children too soon, lying more, dying more, crying more, buying more, and parents saying more and more, "what's the use? They ain't listening to nothing we say, "let's go get stoned!"

*The unemployed are saying it! The current administration has done all it can to continue dismantling the union movement in this country, while at the same time allowing major industries like the automobile, steel, shipbuilding, and electronics to locate overseas. So, the unemployed are saying, "what's the use, we might as well..."

*Congress is saying it! Clearly one-third of the current elected members of the House are likely to be defeated in the November elections, or have retired because of the House Banking scandal. So, if not in word, then at least, in deed , they are saying, "let's go get stoned!"

 *The lonely are saying it! In 1992, 85% of the homicide victims in Baltimore, and 93% of those killed in Washington DC were either single, separated, or divorced. So, the agony of being alone and lonely—which used to be just a burden on your mind—has now become a danger to your life!! So, the lonely and alone are saying, "let's go get stoned!"

*The African-American Church is saying it! The Black Church has institutionalized the worship of White males; enthroned doing for God out of duty, instead of love; while creating an arena of philosophical fragmentation, value dislocation, and spiritual desti-tution. Is it any wonder many Christians don't wait 'till Commun-ion Sunday to get their wine; but stop on their way home and say, "let's go get stoned!"

(That brings me to my text.)

While today's church finds it necessary to go get stoned; the early church had to defend itself against the charge of being drunk in church! When Peter stood to address the astonished people of Jerusalem on the Day of Pentecost, he began his statement with the words, "these men are not drunk as ye suppose! What you see is not because of wine-drinking! Why, it is only 8am and the liquor stores aren't open, yet! This is the Holy Ghost! This is what Joel was trying to tell you way back in 740 BC, that there was coming a day when the people of God were going to empty themselves of the wine of this world, and get filled with a new wine—the Holy

Spirit! Everybody else is going to wish they were drunk; but the only way they can save their life is to call on the name of the Lord, Jesus Christ."

(Isn't it sad that the modern church is not even accused of being drunk? Even if we were, there would not be enough evidence to indict or convict us!) Those in the Upper Room honestly thought the apostles were either drunk or mad, or both. While, the church of today doesn't live under any such cloud of suspicion—that's not a reason to smile, it's cause to cry. If we lived a little closer to our faith, we, too, would need to answer the suspicions that our behavior aroused; we'd have to defend ourselves against the charge of being tipsy or stoned.

What are the marks of someone being drunk? Not deaddrunk and argumentative like some people get, but inebriated. We use such words as gay, jolly, hearty, exhilarated, exuberant, to describe them. The Greeks had a good word for someone in that condition, "euphoric"—which means having an immense feeling of well-being. Mind you, whenever one gets euphoric from strong drink, the feeling is a false one: it sends you straight up, only to drop you back down!

But, while under the influence you forget your troubles, have a sense of expansiveness to everyone, and for a while feel the world is a wonderful place to be.

Trouble is "the night before" is seldom worth "the morning after!" It is why the best drunk loathes to look at themselves in the mirror, and remember the depths of degradation they sank to, while getting stoned.

There is a way to get "high," and stay that way! The cost of this fix is already paid, too! You see, knowing Jesus gives you real euphoria! He gives the divine indwelling of the Holy Spirit that can make you "run through a troop, and jump over a wall." Jesus makes your burden lighter, and will brighten up your darkest night. If you have him in your life, he'll take the load off your mind, and put it on his shoulders. Didn't he tell us, "come unto me, all ye that labor and are heavy laden, and I will give you rest. Take my yoke upon you, and learn of me, for my yoke is easy, and my burden is light."

Is it any wonder the disciples acted like they were drunk,

when they realized Jesus had sent just what he promised—the Lord ascended, and the Holy Ghost descended! That's what made them so gay and joyful!

*The Holy Ghost came down—they wouldn't have to be lonely again.

*The Holy Ghost came down—they could heal the sick and raise the dead.

*The Holy Ghost came down—they could open blinded eyes.

The experience of our brothers, then, teaches us three (3) things about being drunk on the Holy Ghost: First: *It will give you a loosend tongue.*

One of the sure signs of intoxication is people start talking freely. That's what happened on Pentecost! A few hours earlier, the disciples had been scared of their own shadows. Not one of them would dare say anything about Jesus. But, when the Holy Ghost got a hold on them, they just couldn't keep it to themselves!

In addition, there was the added dimension that people from different nations could understand what they were saying, even though the Disciples spoke with the Galilean accent. Today, we have a lot of folk in the church who will spread gossip, but, not the gospel. There is not a surer sign of the powerlessness of God's people than the fact they talk about everything, and everybody, but God!

But, when the Holy Spirit comes into your life, you'll want to talk about nothing and no one, but the Lord. All of us can't be eloquent and powerful and deep; but that's alright. Somebody said, "If you cannot preach like Peter, and you cannot pray like Paul, you can tell the love of Jesus, you can say he died to save us all." I don't know how you feel about it; but, I believe Charles Wesley was right, when he said,

> "Oh for a thousand tongues to sing,
> my great Redeemers praise.
> The glory of my God and King,
> the triumphs of His grace.
> My gracious Master and my God
> assist me to proclaim, to spread
> through all the earth abroad the
> glories of thy name.

Jesus, the name that calms our fears,
and sets the prisoner free. His blood
can make the foulest clean; His blood
availed for me.
(but, I can't stop singing 'till I get to this verse)
Hear him ye deaf, His praise ye dumb,
your loosened tongues employ.
Ye blind behold your Savior come,
And leap ye lame for joy."

The second lesson is: being high on the Holy Ghost—like being intoxi-cated—can make you face your fears.
Before the Holy Ghost, they were just a rag-tag bunch of lonely, fearful, and dejected brothers. But, when they got some holy glide in their stride and some heavenly pep in their step, they were able to face their fears, their enemies, and their tomorrows:
*John was banished on an Isle called Patmos, but he was still able to see visions and write the Book of Revelation.
*While Stephen was being stoned to death, he looked towards heaven, and prayed, "lay this charge not to them." (He must have been stoned!).
*Paul suffered like none of the others, he received "40 stripes, minus one, five times he was stoned; three times shipwrecked; in journeying often; in perils of waters, robbers in the city and in the country; in perils at sea and on land; in weariness and painfulness often; and hunger and thirst much; and cold; lonely, and naked..."
But, he stayed so high on the Lord, that he said:
"If I must boast, then I will boast on my
infirmities. I knew a man once,
who was caught up into the third heaven,
where he heard things unspeakable
which is not lawful for man to utter.
And less I should be exalted above measure,
there was given to me a thorn in the flesh..."
(I'm a witness: if you get high on the Holy Ghost you can thrive in the faith, though you've got a thorn in the flesh) And he said,
"I sought the lord for this thing three times,
but God said to me, "my grace, is sufficient
for thee, for my strength is made perfect in

weakness. Therefore, I will pleasure in
my infirmities, in reproaches, in necessities,
in being cast down, for when I am weak,
then I am strong."

*The final lesson this text teaches is: when you get high on the Holy Ghost,
you can't hide your joy!* When the Holy Spirit came upon those
men, it swept them into a state of absolute euphoria—their speech
betrayed their hearts, and their joy came bursting forth. That's
what happens when a sinner finds the Lord—they feel they can
walk on air! They start singing at the oddest times! When you
get wrapped up, tied up, and tangled up in Jesus, it's a fermenta-
tion of the heart, and an intoxication of the soul. Even now, "when
I think of the goodness of Jesus, and all he's done for me, my soul
cries, "hallelujah, thank God for saving me." (can I testify?):

"I was sinking deep in sin,
far from the peaceful shore,
very deeply stained within,
sinking to rise no more,
but the Master of the sea,
heard my despairing cry,
from the water lifted me,
now safe am I.
Love lifted me, love lifted me,
when nothing else would help,
love lifted me."

(Can I testify?)

"And, He walks with me, and He
talks with me, and He tells me
I am His own; and the joy we
share as we tarry there, none
other has ever known..."

(Can I testify?)

"This joy I have, the world didn't give it to me,
and the world can't take it away..."

(THE DOOR OF THE CHURCH IS OPEN...)

"Back To The Future"

(This sermon was preached at Unity UMC on Sunday, January 3, 1993.)

Acts 2:1-7, 12-17   (Text 2:16)

Last week, I had the privilege of visiting some of the great and historical sites from the Civil Rights Era that are located in the state of Alabama. I was blessed to see the famous Dexter Avenue Baptist Church, the church Dr. Martin Luther King, Jr. pastored while he led the Montgomery Bus Boycott. I saw the famous Alabama State House where Governor George Wallace wrote many of his famous "segregation forever" speeches. I visited the famous Brown's Chapel AME Church in Selma, where the march from Selma to Montgomery was planned and began.

As I stood with my wife, Rev. Carolyn Handy, and Dr. Kay Pace at the foot of the Edmund Pettus Bridge—where those vicious racist attacked the marchers on that infamous "Bloody Sunday" in 1965—a deep and startling chill went through my body. This chill did not emanate from the weather, for it was a balmy 70+ degrees. It came, rather, from the startling and stark realization that in the almost 30 years since the infamous march across that bridge occurred, we as a people have made tremendous strides and progress in many areas; but, at the same time, in many other ways things are just as bad, or worse! For instance:
*The desks in too many of our inner-city schools are still pupiled by the faces of only one race;
*Most African-Americans are still trying to grab hold of the first rung of the economic ladder;
*The infant mortality rate for African-American babies in America is still higher than some third-world countries;
*Too many of our street corners are populated by men and women who have, seemingly, failed at the game of life, and thrown in the towel; I went to revisit the past, and I saw (all too clearly) the future—and I didn't like what I saw!

Things have gotten progressively worse in too many areas.

Oh, don't get me wrong, we have made tremendous strides:

*Those were Black boys running the football up and down the field for the University of Alabama in the Sugar Bowl. That is progress.

*Black astronauts are manning space capsules in outer space. That signifies progress, too.

*More African-Americans are serving in cabinet-level positions in our nation's government, than ever before—that is truly progress. But these are merely cosmetic coverings on an otherwise dreary situation. When you get right down to it, our negative past is slowly but surely becoming our dismal future. In other words, I think it behooves us to look at this Back To The Future business with keener and closer scrutiny, for I believe some things in the past were bad and need to be left there. But; other things about the past can serve to help us with our future, and if we know them, we don't have to make the same mistakes tomorrow, we made yesterday. (Notice, I didn't say, "we won't," I said, "we don't have to...")

We are prepared to launch into this year with a brand new crew of officers at the helm of the good ship, "Unity." Many of last year's crew have returned to the status of being passengers, after doing a fine job. Others remain at the helm, along with the new crew, facing the uncharted waters of 1993, looking to sail to higher heights and greater glories in the Lord, Jesus Christ. And here's where Back To The Future comes in:

 *We know from last year loose lips, sink ships. In other words, spreading gossip kills, spreading the Gospel saves;

*We know from last year prayer changes things; and prayer changes people, too;

*We learned not to wait until we're in trouble to call on the Lord, but, to call on Him now—when we don't need him, and he'll be there when we do;

*We know from the past year that Paul was right, when he said in Galations 6:7, "whatever a man soweth, that shall he reap". In other words, if you're stingy and "niggardly" in your giving to God, don't look for the windows (or even the peepholes) of heaven to open up for you.

Oh, it is Back To The Future for us, this year. For if we

learn from our past (back), then our sailing on the good ship, Unity (our future) will be brighter, and our burdens will be lighter.

In our text, this morning, Dr. Luke gives us yet another understanding of Back To The Future. The disciples have been required by Jesus to gather in the same Upper Room where He had instituted the Lord's Supper, and broke bread with them. They were afraid of the Jews and feared they might be killed, too. So, it's easy to understand why all of them were there.

In addition, it is the celebration of the Feast of Weeks which marked the 50 days it had taken that ragtag group of foot-weary travelers to get from Egypt to Mt. Sinai, and receive the Ten-Commandments. And, there were many other Jews with them.

> (And that line speaks volumes to us as we start this year: if we are faithful and obedient to God in celebrating our special days, we won't have to worry about drawing a crowd. People will come from far and near to see the excitement, if we are excited about what our church is doing for God!)

As they prayed on one accord, my Bible tells me an unusual and unexpected "happening" took place. Suddenly, a sound from heaven filled the house. God had decided to make a personal appearance on the "Good Morning, Israel Show." There was a blur on their mental screens and the picture became distorted—so much so that they saw men with fire dancing on their heads.

If that wasn't enough, the folk they were watching began to talk in such a way everybody understood them, even though everyone in the place spoke a different language! Well, that was too much for them! Nobody had acted like this before in all of their goings and comings to the synagogue:

*the Priest didn't talk like that;
*the Scribes wouldn't talk like that;
*the Sadducees couldn't talk like that; and,
*the Levites should've talked like that.

Only one thing could make men talk like that: They Must Be Drunk! Peter stands up and sets the record straight. He said, (and I paraphrase, here):

> "They can't be drunk, 'cause it's only 9 o'clock in the morning, and the liquor stores ain't open yet."

He went on to say, "This (the future) is that (the past) which was spoken of by the prophet, Joel."
If you want to understand this phenomena, you have to go backwards to do so—you've got to go Back To The Future!

When the Holy Spirit came in their midst, they were changed from a rag-tag group of frightened men, to a powerful theophany of God working in their midst. And every time the Holy Ghost shows up in a crowd watch it transform them from being moral midgets to spiritual giants.

*He showed up in a desert one day, and folk who were lost found "a pillar of cloud by day and a pillar of fire by night" to guide them.

*He showed up at a king's banquet one night, and began to write on a wall, "Mene, Mene, Tekal Uparshin: thou hast been weighed in the balances and found wanting."

*He showed up on a mountain one day. Though the odds were 450 to one against him, the prophet, Elijah was able to slay the enemy and still had enough energy to outrun a chariot back to town.

*He showed up on a hillside one day, and though there were only two fish, and five barley loaves, he opened up a "supermarket on the hillside," and fed 5,000 men, women, boys and girls and still had 12 baskets of leftovers to take to the "Synagogue Soup Kitchen" in town.

*He showed up at a graveyard one day:
  -although Pilate stationed 120 soldiers in front of the grave...,
  -although there was a two-ton rock placed over it...
  -despite all these barriers...

Early Easter morning:
  -before the sun rose over the Eastern hills...
  -before the rooster gave his early morning wake up call...
  -before the women could get to the tomb to anoint his body...

Jesus was raised from the dead, stood out on resurrection rock, and declared "all power in Heaven and in earth is given unto me!"
Yes, when the Holy Ghost shows up, things are changed, people are changed, situations are changed, churches are changed, preachers are changed, choirs are changed, ushers are changed, meetings are changed, committees are changed, boards are changed, worshipers are changed, offerings are changed. Yes, when the Holy

Ghost shows up, even sermons are changed!
*when the Holy Ghost comes, failure turns to success,
*when the Holy Ghost comes, despair turns to hope,
*when the Holy Ghost comes, sorrow turns to joy,
*when the Holy Ghost comes, pessimism becomes optimism,
*when the Holy Ghost comes, fear turns to bravery,
*when the Holy Ghost comes, midnight is turned to midday,
*when the Holy Ghost comes, water breaks forth in the desert, lonely hearts are made glad, nightmares become sweet dreams. When the Holy Ghost shows up, things that seemed impossible, turn out to be "a piece of cake."
Here at Unity—by looking back at what happened in the past—we know a better future is guaranteed for us if we keep the Holy Ghost in our prayers, the Holy Ghost in our conversation, the Holy Ghost in our meetings, the Holy Ghost in our homes, the Holy Ghost in our walk, in our talk, in our glide and in our stride. This is Back To The Future for us!

Finally, the reason the Holy Ghost came to those disciples is because they were doing what God told them to do: Be On One Accord! My beloved:
*I don't know how you feel about it, but I want more accord in our singing;
*I don't know how you feel about it, but I want more accord on our Usher Board;
*I don't know how you feel about it, but I want more accord in our Men's Group;
*I don't know how you feel about it, but I want more accord in our Women's Group;
*I don't know how you feel about it, but I want more accord on our Finance Committee;
*I don't know how you feel about it, but I want more accord in our Communion Stewards;
*I don't know how you feel about it, but I want more accord amongst our Kitchen Crew;
In the spirit of Sankofa, let us use what is good from the past, to help us make the future better.
In the words of the song-poet, we should all be saying:
        "Come holy spirit, heavenly dove,

with all thy quickening power;
and kindle a flame of sacred love,
in these cold hearts of ours."
We should all be saying:
Spirit of the living God,
fall afresh on me.
Spirit of the living God,
fall afresh on me.
Melt me, mold me, fill me, use me.
Spirit of the living God,
fall afresh on me."
Yes! All of us need to say:
"Let it breathe on me,
Let it breathe on me ,
Let the breathe of the Lord, now breathe on me..."
I'm going Back To The Future:
*I'm going back to prayer, so I can get more power in the future.
*I'm going back to grace, so I can get more mercy in the future.
*I'm going back to salvation, so I can get more justification in the future.
*I'm going back to the rock, so I can get some blessed assurance in the future.
*I'm going back to Jesus, so I can get some joy in the future.
*I'm going back to the Holy Ghost, so I can get direction for my life, this ministry, and our church.
I don't know where you're going this year, but I'm going Back To The Future:
"I moved from my old house,
I moved from my old friends,
I moved from my old way of life, thank God,
I moved out to a brand new life.
Can't you see I got a new walk?
Can't you see I got a new way?
And one day I'll live in that new land, thank God,
I moved out to a brand new life."

(THE DOOR OF THE CHURCH IS OPEN…)

"You Are Hereby Summoned To Be A Witness"

(This sermon was preached at Unity UMC on February 14, 1993 for Black History Month.)

Luke 24:36-53

Someone once asked Dr. Howard Thurman, that great Black theologian, what was wrong with the world? Dr. Thurman thought for a while, and replied (tongue in cheek), "I dunno, I guess it's people."

Though said in jest, Dr. Thurman may have hit upon the supernal problem with our world—people. Think about it: in some ways this planet would be a lot better off, if it weren't for people. How many hearts are broken, how many plans aborted, how much misery is caused, how many deaths, suicides, waste, and war occurs simply because people are unable to get along with other people. You see this problem everywhere, from the playground to the board room, from Roland Park to Harlem Park, from the White House to the outhouse, to the church house—the problem is not the program or the plan, it is the man or the woman—it is people!

Many of you have realized that our problems are not drugs, or crime, or money, or jobs, or housing, or wars, or hunger—no, no! Our problem is the way people do or don't handle them. Throughout history, social savants have dreamed of the perfect society for people. Plato described his ideal society in Utopia, Samuel Butler laid out his ideas in Erehwon ("nowhere" spelled backwards.) John Stuart Mill wrote about his in Political Economy, Karl Marx in Das Kapital, and Henry David Thoreau in Walden's Pond. Even Dr. Martin Luther King, Jr. tried to tell us about his perfect society in the "I Have A Dream" speech. But every one of their dreams turned to ashes because of the problem of human relationships. It's easy to put the perfect society on paper; but, it's something else when we transfer those plans from paper to personalities. For when we do, we find human nature with all of it's greed, pride, jealousy, and just plain meanness staring us in the face.

There are two different and distinct views on how to handle our human dilemma. *One view is that we humans will never be dif-*

ferent from our most base forms of thinking and behavior. Those who hold that view also believe that people must be held down, controlled, policed, and governed with an iron hand. It is why there always have been—and will be—totalitarian governments like Hitler's Germany, South Africa's Apartheid, Papa Doc's regime in Haiti, and America's peculiar institution called Chattel Slavery.

The other view is: people can—and must—change! That is the optimistic view. That is the view that Jesus held, too. He believed through the process of learning, people can be transformed and redeemed. It is the reason he was so clear and specific in his appearances to the disciples after his resurrection. He wanted them to do one thing more than anything else—help people to change their lot and circumstances, just as he had helped them to do.

Do you want to know which commandment was the most important to Jesus? It is the one that appears in all four of the Gospels! And, the one commandment that appears in all four Gospels and the Book of Acts is the Great Commission. This was so special to him, he issued a special proclamation:

> "I've done all that I could do in the time I had.
> I spent all my time trying to help people find
> a better way to live. Now, I've got a specific
> job for you. I'm summoning you to appear
> all over this world as a witness to what can
> happen when people follow my directions.
> I want you to preach and teach everywhere you
> can that through repentance and the remission
> of sins, folk can find a better way of life."

In other words, Jesus Christ is the only way and truth through which Metanoia—the word means to change one's mind—can be achieved. So, he deputized his boys to go out and round up as many sheep as possible, and bring them into the fold.

*What was John, the Baptist, doing down at the Jordan River? Preaching and teaching about repentance.

*What was Jesus doing at the Wedding Feast of Cana, and his visits to his hometown of Nazareth? Preaching and teaching about repentance.

*What did he talk about in his Sermon on the Mount, and during those visits He made to Capernaum and Galilee? He talked, preached, and taught about repentance.

*What did Jesus mean when he talked about the Prodigal Son, the Lost Coin, or the Pearl of Great Price? He was talking about repentance.

*And, when he was dying on the cross—his hands and feet nailed, a hole in his side, a crown of thorns on his head—what did he say? "Father, forgive them..." He was talking about repentance.

In over seven major evangelism campaigns, Jesus taught and showed the disciples how to go into the world and convert people's hearts to the way, the truth, and the life. His final act was to commission them to do the same thing. In order for them to perform their mission, he taught them three forms of evangelism:

*Oikos—proselytizing your family and relatives.

*Personal—proselytizing an individual; and,

*Mass—proselytizing a group.

Beloved, I admonish you: if you really want to see Unity live up to its past glory, and its' future potential, then take this summons of Jesus Christ seriously! Be a witness for the Lord! Get up, go out, and be an evangelist—tell somebody the good news: "if anyone be in Christ, they are a new creation, behold old things pass away, all things become new."

I hear somebody's spirit saying, "well, Harlem Park Preacher, that's easy for others; but, I don't know the Bible like my brother or sister." Even if you don't know it as good as somebody else, you can learn! Come to Bible Study, come to prayer meeting, come to Noon Day Ministry on Friday's. You can comply with the commission, even if you don't know scripture that well. "How?" (I'm so glad you asked.) *You can be a witness by stressing the positive, instead of the negative!*

People in church spend too much time talking about what's wrong: what's wrong with the preacher, what's wrong with the choir, what's wrong with the finance committee, what's wrong with this, what's wrong with that! Negative Christianity is no Christianity at all. Paul said it in Philippians 4:8,

> "whatever things are pure, whatsoever things are just,
> whatsoever things are pure, whatsoever things are lovely,
> whatsoever things are of good report, if there be any
> virtue, and if there be any praise, think on these things."

In other words, you've got to accent the positive, eliminate the negative, and don't mess with "Mr. Inbetween."

The second thing you can do is: appreciate more than criticize! For every "put down" Jesus uttered—like the one against the Pharisees when he said, "woe, unto ye hypocrites,ye make clean the outside of the cup and platter, but inwardly ye are like graveyards, full of dead men's bones..."; he uttered a hundred "praises" of people. In fact, he always seemed to be blessing people: "blessed are the poor in spirit, those who mourn, the meek, the hungry, and the thirsty for righteousness, the merciful, the pure in heart, the peacemakers..."

The truth is: not many of those he said those things to, were what he called them—humble, poor in spirit, meek, and so forth. But, Jesus was the master psychologist. He *appreciated* them into being just how he described them.

We, too, can bring out the best in people, if we appreciate them more than we put them down. Jesus knew we were all the things we humans are: weak, mean, stingy, cowards, haters; but, he didn't call us those things! He called us "children of God..." Doesn't the word say, "now, we are the children of God, and it doth not yet appear what we shall be; but, when he shall appear, then we shall be like him?"

Don't get it twisted—I am for real! I know there is some wrong in every one of us; but, suppose we could find something in everyone to praise them about! (As Dr. Walter Amprey, our former Superintendent of Schools was often heard to say, "catch them doing something good!") Can you imagine what that would do for our co-workers, for our wives and husbands, for our children, our neighbors, or our brothers and sisters in Christ!?! If we would find something to praise folk about, what a different world it would be:
*the six o'clock news wouldn't be so dreary;
*the newspaper would bring a smile, instead of a sigh;
*our homes would be a place where people delight to come;
*our church would be a church—not just a crowd!

That's what Paul was talking about in 1 Corinthians 13, when he said, "though I speak with the tongues of angels, and have not love, I am but a sounding brass and a tinkling cymbal."

A Voice In The Wilderness

Third—*We can be a witness for Christ by teaching: the quality of our inner character is more important than the quality of our outer possessions.* It is a travesty, it's a shame the world knows Christianity better for its conspicuous consumption, than for its witness for the one whose name we bear! Jesus was more concerned about what was in us, than what was on us! You remember when he said, "what doth it profit a man, if he gain the whole world, and lose his soul?" (You remember, don't you?) You remember when he said, "seek ye first the kingdom of heaven, and all its righteousness, and all these things shall be added unto you?"

You may not plan to do any evangelizing; but, your life is a witness for something. You're either an ambassador for Christ, or an "imp for evil." I don't care who you are, or where you went to school; whether you went to Morgan, Morehouse, or nobody's house—somebody is watching you to see if there's anything worthwhile about this man called Jesus. I don't care who you are, or what you do in life, you're going to be a witness! You're either a witness for Jesus, or you'll be a witness against him! But, you are going to be a witness!

Last week, I received a call from an agent of the Drug Enforcement Agency. He said, "Dr. Handy, would you testify in court against the notorious night club, called The Underground. Nobody else will come forward to speak, so we can keep this place from being turned over to other drug dealers." I said, "but, Sir, I have never been in the place, and I surely don't know any of the patrons—they don't hang in my concentric circle of friends." And, he said, "but, all we need you to do is testify about what was going on around the place." As I prepared this message, I thought about that call. Isn't that what Jesus wants us to do, when he says, "ye shall be my witnesses?"

*You and I weren't there when he walked the dusty roads of Palestine;

*You and I weren't there when he raised the dead, gave sight to the blind, or made the lame to walk;

*You and I weren't there when he made the winds and the waves obey his will;

*You and I weren't there when he fed 5,000 with only a little boy's bag-lunch;

*You and I weren't there when they made him carry his cross, receive the thorns on his head, the spear, in his side, or when they nailed him to a tree;

*You and I weren't there when he got up from the grave on that first Easter Morning, and said, "all power in heaven and in earth is given unto me."

But, you and I can tell what we have seen since we've been around the Holy Spirit of the man, named Jesus:

*we can say, "He woke me up this morning, and started me on my way;

*we can say, "He put bread on my table, and clothes on my back;

*we can say, "He saved my soul, one day, and made me whole;

*we can say, "He gives me peace in the midst of a storm;

*we can say, "He walks with me, and he talks with me, and he tells me I am his own; and the joy we share, as we tarry there, none other has ever known."

That's right, you and I weren't there; but, in the words of the song poet, we can say:

> "At the cross, at the cross, where I first saw
> the light and the burdens of my heart rolled
> away. It was there by faith, I received my
> sight, and now I am happy all the day."

As African-American History Month, 1993, begins, the world lost one of its most prolific and famous composers of gospel music, Thomas A. Dorsey. As the story goes, "Old Barrel House Tom" (as he was known before he began to sing and write gospel music) had gotten married, and had a new baby.

He and his family were traveling on the back roads of Mississippi, when suddenly, blinding lights came over the hill, and a bunch of drunk, White boys ran into their car, killing his wife and baby. Those racist wouldn't even take his wife and child to the hospital! They told him, "get on nigger, you had no business out here at night." So, Tom left his wife and child and started walking to get help. As he walked, he began thinking about his loss. The more he walked, the more he cried, and soon the words—which have inspired millions of burdened and broken hearts—came leaping from the depths of his soul:

> "Precious Lord, take my hand, lead me

on, let me stand. I am tired, I am weak,
I am worn. Through the storm, through
the night, lead me on, to the light, take
my hand, precious Lord, and lead me home."

Oops, There it is! You are summoned to tell somebody not what you read, not what you heard, but what God has done for you! And, "if you cannot preach like Peter, and you cannot pray like Paul, you can tell the love of Jesus. You can say he died to save us all."

You Are Hereby Summoned To Be A Witness:

*tell somebody—if you're sick or in sin, I know a man from Galilee, who will set you free;"

*tell somebody—my doctor has more medicine in the hem of his garment, than all the drugstores in town;

*tell somebody—it doesn't matter which side of the tracks you may have come from—the right or the wrong side. Once you come to Christ, you will be on the right track!

*tell somebody who is down and out, or up and over:

"Come ye disconsolate, where 'ere we languish,
come to the mercy seat, fervently kneel.
Here bring your wounded hearts, here tell
your anguish. Earth has no sorrow, that heaven
cannot heal."

(THE DOOR OF THE CHURCH IS OPEN...)

"5 SMOOTH STONES"

(This sermon was preached at Unity UMC on October, 1, 1993.)

In his book, THE INNER EAR, David Smalls gives some marvelous insights about one of our societal problems. Dr. Smalls believes—and I concur—the growing, ongoing conflict, the alarming amount of animosity, and the heightened hostility existing in our society is because we humans have forgotten how to listen to each other.

Dr. Smalls thinks this lost art—more than any other factor—is why there is so much violence and death in our families, our cities, and our nation. Even more interesting, he says the cause of this decline in our ability to listen to one another is we are a society of automatons—our listening skills have declined in proportion to the amount of time we spend "watching" TV, movies, and videos.

There seems to be many holes in Dr. Smalls theory. After our emotional reaction subsides, however, we may have more to agree with—than to disagree about! Dr. Smalls thinks when we only had radio and the spoken word, there was no way we could understand something, unless we paid rapt attention, and "listened" with our whole heart and mind. TV's, movies, and videos, he goes on, have removed the requirement that we listen to get the picture (do you get the picture?)

*What does a baby want when it cries? To be listened to!

*What does a parent want when they're telling their children something? To be listened to!

*What does a teacher want when they're teaching? To be listened to!

*What does a husband or a wife want when they're talking? To be listened to!

*What does a friend want when they call or engage you in a face to face conversation? To be listened to!

*What does a choir want when they're singing, or a preacher want when they're preaching? To be listened to!

One outcome of Dr. Small's theory is: if we can't, or don't, or won't listen (with our whole heart, mind and soul) to what is being said or sung on Sunday, then we fail to have a meaningful relationship with our worshiping neighbors. And, if we fail to have a meaningful relationship with our neighbor, then it follows, (ipso facto—as night follows day!) we fail to have meaningful worship of God! Oh, I believe you can worship God in your own tent door; but, when you do, if you are not listening, you leave that moment worse, not better, too!

Dr. Smalls also states that quality listening requires three things we must practice until perfect. He believes to be a quality listener you must know the ethos, pathos, and the logos of the speaker. In order to understand what is being said in a sermon, sung in a song, or spoken in a statement, you must know:
*the character of the speaker—the ethos,
*the feelings behind what is being said—the pathos; and,
*the intent or meaning of what is being talked about—the logos.
Leave out any of these factors, and true communion between the speaker and listener cannot exist. For, whenever people talk, that is what they are trying to establish—communion! So, if you and I want to do some quality listening to the story in our text, we need to examine the ethos, pathos, and logos of it.

The principle character in our story, this morning, is David, a man about whom we know a great deal:
*we know he is the son of Jesse,
*we know he is one of several sons Jesse has,
*we know he is a shepherd by profession,
*we know he is ruddy in complexion—meaning he has red or rustic coloring to his skin; and,
*we know he is a musician, songwriter, and singer. (He will become king of Israel; but, that doesn't occur until later.)
*we also know David's character is different from the other members of his family, and the other men of Israel. For when the giant, Goliath, came upon the Israelites—unlike other men who cowered in fear—David said, "who is this uncircumcised Philistine, who dares to tease the armies of the living God of Israel?"

What he said shows me David was not afraid to stand out in the crowd—to dare and be different!

It is a lot to say about anyone's character: they aren't afraid to stand up and stand out in the crowd. One of our society's biggest problems is too many of us strive hard to be part of the crowd, to be accepted. It is a major factor contributing to the teen and gang violence on our city's streets! Because our young people want—and are trying—to be accepted, because "everyone wants to fit in where they can get in, and get in where they can fit in," everyone wants to conform. This drive to belong is what drives our young people to join gangs!

But, the Christian religion is a religion of non-conformity! You can't be a good Christian and be like the world. You can't even be a good Christian and fit into the church—you have got to stand up for what is right, even when the crowd is going the other way.

In the late 1960's, I was was attending a football game at Fulton County Stadium between the Washington Football Team and the Atlanta Falcons. On my way to the stadium, I passed a protest march on Peachtree Street. All of the protesters were part of the "beat generation." They were carrying signs and placards which read "down with conformity;" and yet, almost everyone of their signs were identical. In fact, their clothes were identical, their hair style was identical, their shoes were identical, their talk was identical—they even smelled identical. Although they were dropping out, they were still trying to fit in!

Beloved, you can't please God and mammon! You've got to stand up for God, or you'll fall for anything! That's the ethos of the story and of David—he was a man who stood up for God.

The second key to critical listening is to know the Pathos, the feelings being communicated by the speaker. And unless you have absolutely no "bowels of compassion" as Paul calls them, unless your heart is as cold as a well-diggers hands in Montana, then when you read this story, you must feel some fear and anxiety for this lad as he goes out to face the giant, Goliath.

But, be careful that "feeling" something is not all you take away from the experience:

Dr. Martin Luther King Jr. tells the story of a woman, worshiping at Dexter Ave Church while he was preaching, one morning. As she came through the fellowship line, she told him, "Rev, that was a powerful sermon you preached this morning." Dr. King asked her, "What did you like about it?" (or what was the sermon about?) The sister replied, "I don't know, all I know is it made me feel good."

Brothers and sisters, if you want to go away from church with just a good feeling that's fine—at least you're not going away empty-handed. But, if you listen, if you listen with your whole heart, mind, and soul, you'll get a whole lot more!

David was clear about his feelings. He didn't want his people embarrassed or afraid of Goliath. So, guided by his feelings of empathy and concern for his people, he risked his life to save the day. He faced that giant unafraid because: not only did he care; but, God cared, too! God had feelings about this situation too!

That's the lesson he's trying to teach: No matter what giant you're facing—the giant of sickness, of a broken heart, of death, the giant of loneliness, of trouble in your marriage, problems with your children—whatever or whoever the giant:

"Be not dismayed, what'er betide,
God will take care of you.
Beneath his wings of love abide,
God will take care of you
God will take care of you,
through every day, o'er all the way
He will take care of you, God will take care of you."

*You've got to understand the Ethos—the character of the one who's speaking.

*You've got to let the Pathos—the feelings—of the message or the messenger speak to you; and finally, *you need to understand the Logos, the content of what is being said!*

The Logos of this text teaches us we need to have some tools or some weapons when we fight the giants of this world! If you listen, you'll see that David's story is not just about an event in history! No, no! When the Word says David bent down and picked up those 5 Smooth Stones, I believe he was picking up more than mere earthly material. I believe he picked some stones —that he learned from God—would help in the time of testing.

All of us have challenges to face in life. My family is going through the pain of losing it's patriarchal leader, and we are facing the giant of grief, today. You may be going through something in your own life! You may be facing some giant which seems too big to conquer by yourself, because of its size and proportions.

I just stopped by Unity to tell you: don't give up, and don't give out! The Logos of this text teaches me that we have the same stones available to us that David had. What were those stones?

The first stone was Faith. David had enough faith that the God of Israel would see him through this crisis.

The second stone he picked up was Hope. David had seen what God could do for him when he had to wrestle a lion and a bear with only his hands. So, David had a heart full of Hope, that God would see him through, one more time. I can almost hear him saying as he bends down to pick up that second stone:

"My hope is built on nothing less,
Than Jesus' blood and righteousness.
I dare not trust the sweetest frame,
But wholly lean on Jesus' name..."

The third stone he stooped and scooped was the stone of Love. David loved the people of Israel with all his heart. He loved his brothers with all his heart, and it was love that gave him the courage and strength to stand up, when everyone else was afraid. Isn't that what sees us through when times are tight, and friends are few? The song poet said:

"The love of God will always be there for,
The love of God is everywhere."

The fourth stone David put in his arsenal was the stone of Prayer.. Can't you hear him saying in his heart:

"Just a little talk with Jesus,
and I'll tell him all about my troubles,
he will hear me when I cry,
and he'll answer by and by.
("yeah, everything is alright now, 'cause")
I can feel a little prayer wheel turning,
and I know a little fire is burning.
Just a little talk with Jesus makes everything alright."

Finally, I see David holding that fifth rock in his hand, and turning it over and over. As he examines it. I can hear him saying "this looks like an old rock I've seen before—it must be the Rock of Ages. This looks like the stone that the builders rejected—I'd best not leave this one. This looks like Jesus!"

(Here's what I want to leave with you, today):

*If you want to fight the good fight of faith…

*If you want to be an over-comer…

*If you want to gain the heights over your adversary, then you need to get the "Rock of Ages" in your life!

He was just a lowly shepherd boy who didn't have much, but he had Christ! I can hear him saying:

"I don't possess houses or lands,
Fine clothes or jewelry.
Sorrows and cares in this ol' world
My lot seems to be;
But I have a Christ all in my life,
That makes me happy.
And Christ is all, all and all, this world to me."

I can hear him saying:

"Oh, it is Jesus, Oh it is Jesus,
It's Jesus in my soul.
For I have touched the hem of his garment,
And his love has made me whole."

I can hear him saying as he slings that rock:

"Jesus is all the world to me, my life, my joy, my all.
I go to him for blessings and he gives them o'er and o'er.
When I am sad, to him I go.
No other one can cheer me so.
When I am sad, he makes me glad. He's my friend."

What's your giant, today? The giant of sickness? The giant of heartache? The giant of…

Whatever your obstacle is, try Jesus, he satisfies:

*He's like Pepsi-Cola—He's the real thing.

*He's like Ford—have you tried Him lately?

*He's like Hallmark Cards—He cared enough to send the very best.

"There's not a friend, like the lowly Jesus,
No not one, no not one.

One who can heal all your soul's diseases—
No, not one; no not one.
Jesus knows all about our troubles,
He will guide 'till the day is done.
There's not a friend like the lowly Jesus—
No, not one; no not one!"

(THE DOOR OF THE CHURCH IS OPEN...)

Councilmen Abayomi, Edward Reisinger, & Melvin Stukes register as candidates for City Council in 1999.

Dr Henry Louis (Skip) Gates, Minister Michael Carter, Dr Abayomi

Groundbreaking Ceremony for Edmondson Commons Apartments --
June, 2003, (l-r) Blaise Cook, President, Harkins Builders; Council-
woman Catherine Pugh; Dr. Abayomi; President Sheila Dixon;
Vice-President Agnes Welch; Lt. Gov. Michael Steele; Mayor Martin
O'Mally; Kevin Bell and Bill Stifler, The Bell Group.

Lay Speakers, 2001 (l-r): Wanda Watson, Millicent Rice, Blendie Buie,
Michael Carter, Druscilla Bunch, Carolyn Lee.

74   A Voice In The Wilderness

United Methodist Men, 1999--(l-r): Arthur Hyde, Gregory Gaines, Armstrong Miller, William (Bill) Opher, Avon Burrell, Zannie Jernigan George Cooper-President, Winston Jackson, Charles Green

Finance Committee, 1996: Catherine Green, Dorothy Coleman, Margaret Mason, Chairperson, Larry McNeil, Clara Lane.

Pastor's Aid Ministry, 2002 (l-r): Patricia Jones, Leon Miller, Michelle Flowers, Gladys Nutt, David Mae Redfern, Frances Johnson, Kathaleen Carey, Zannie & Teresa Jernigan; Wanda Watson, Betty Camphor-President, Grace Opher, Dorothy Coleman, Pensla Corbett, Rev. Blanche Slaughter.

UMOJA Mass Choir--2008 (l-r): Gregory Gaines, Millicent Rice, Kathaleen Carey, Michelle Flowers, Patricia Jones, Wanda Watson, Carolyn Lee, James Wise-Musician, Delores Young, Julia Young, Eleanor Cooper, Betty Camphor, Nancy Blake, Anna Palmer, Druscilla Bunch, President.

　　　　A Voice In The Wilderness

The Honorable Reverend Doctor Kwame Osayaba Abayomi

Doorkeepers, 1998 (l-r): Ernestine Harrison, Vernon Camphor, Sr., Teresa Jernigan, Theodore Hudgins-President, David Mae Redfern Vice-President, Pearl Richardson, Candace Smoot, Armstrong Miller.

"A Disturbing Dilemma"

(This sermon was preached at Unity UMC on Easter Sunday, April 16, 1995.)

Matthew 28:1-10

In his book, ADAM, WHERE ARE YOU?, Jawanza Konjufu paints a very disturbing picture of the Black Church. In this seminal work, Konjufu describes the church as being "rich, but foolish with its money; powerful, but wasting its power on riotous living; important, but caught up in being a legend in its' own mind, rather than a legend in its time." He goes on to describe this powerful giant with almost two-billion dollars in annual revenue, and over $90 billion dollars in assets as being careless, cruel, and cantankerous."

The author also points out the reality of the absence of the Black male in the church, and the problem this poses for the Black woman, the Black child, and the Black race, in general. For instance, he says every saved-sister is looking for a BMS, who's a BMW (that's a Black-man-saved, who's a Black-man-working.) Isn't that true? Thank God for those Black men who are in the church; but, look around you this morning. The biggest missing segment of the Black church is the Black man! Where is he?

(Here's the disturbing dilemma):
*He's on the street corner putting dope in his veins, instead of hope in his brains.
*He's home in bed, trying to recover from last night's party.
*He's in prison, or in jail—unavailable to his family for years to come; or,
*He's "missing in action," because he's decided the church is a place for women, weaklings, and wimps.

His thinking contributes to the alarming statistic that the Black church is comprised of 75% females to 25% males. Unless we're going to shift from monogamous to a polygamous lifestyle, I'm afraid too many right-thinking, right-living sisters are gonna be "manless;" unless they're willing to settle for a brother who's unsaved and unemployed, or share a good one with another sister. I know that's a disturbing statement on this Easter Sunday, 1995; but that's why God had me tell you: just like those sisters were disturbed by what they found when they went to the tomb that first Easter morning—God wants us to be disturbed by what we've found, too!

In our text, this morning, we find Mary Magdalene, and the other Mary rushing to the tomb, looking for a man, too. Just like sisters of today, they were not just looking for any man—they were looking for a particular man, they were looking for Jesus. You see, there hadn't been enough time to render the last rites to the body of Jesus because the Sabbath had come, and Jewish law forbade them from doing any work, even burying someone, on the Sabbath.

Now, the Sabbath was over. So, early in the morning, on the first day of the week, they'd set out to find this man, Jesus. When they reached the tomb, they found a disturbing scene: first, there had been, what seemed to be an earthquake. The text says that what really happened was that an angel came down and rolled the stone away from the mouth of the cave.

Now, I need to stop right here for a minute:
Have you ever been in a car accident,
 and when it's all over, you walk away
from that tangled mess of metal with
nothing more than some superficial
scratches on you? Or have you ever
had someone attack you, put the knife
or gun to you and threaten you
with robbery or bodily harm,
and you walk away with nothing but your
nerves shaken?

Has that ever happened to you? If it has, please don't tell anybody that you were lucky. That wasn't luck, that was an angel of God looking out for you. You see:
*I believe in angels—those celestial emissaries who carry messages from God.
*I believe in angels—they're posted by my bedside each and every night...

*I believe in angels—you can't see them, but they're right here in the sanctuary, this morning. Somebody said, "all day, all night, angels keep watching over me."

Well, that's what disturbed these women—an angel had rolled the stone away; and then, as if to add insult to injury, that same angel was now sitting at the mouth of the cave, telling them that Jesus was not here, "He is risen!"

I think these sisters had a right to be disturbed, don't you? For, here, indeed, was A Disturbing Dilemma! The text says that they ran from the graveyard with both fear and joy in their hearts: they were afraid because of what they had seen and heard. They had seen an angel. This angel had performed a miracle, and then stayed around long enough to talk to them. That was cause enough for their fear! But, on top of that the man they had gone looking for was not where he was supposed to be, in the tomb! He was alive!

*They had seen the soldiers drive the nails in his hands.
*They had seen the soldiers drive the spike thru his feet.
*They had seen the spear pierce his side, and the blood and water come gushing from his body.
*They had seen Joseph, of Arimethea beg His body from Pilate, lay it in the tomb, the 36 soldiers placed outside to guard it, and the two-ton stone placed over it.
*They had seen all that! In spite of it, Jesus was risen! He was alive; and, on top of that, they were going to see him again (You see where I'm going with this, don't you?) These women didn't know whether to laugh or cry, to moan or to shout!

That brings me to my first point: Just like Mary Magdalene, women are looking in the wrong place for the missing Black Man! It's not that you don't know how to look for a man, the problem is that many sisters have the wrong image of what a man is when they go searching. (Listen:) whenever the police department wants to find a suspect, they bring in an artist who paints a composite sketch of the person. They take the verbal description and transfer it into a visual! So, this morning, in order to help my sisters in their searching, I want to give you a composite sketch of who you're looking for today.

First, it's not just a man with muscle; he's also a man with a mind.

I'm not talking about how many alphabets a man may have behind his name—no, no! The mind I'm talking about is a mind strong enough not to be swayed by every wind and doctrine; but, supple enough to bend with the winds and fortunes of change. What's wrong with a whole lot of brothers today is they refuse to change with time. There are some things in life that you cannot stop:
*You can't hold back the dawn.
*You cannot stop the incoming tide.
*You can't halt the passage of time; and,
*You cannot stop change from occurring.

I don't mean that you have to go along with every change that comes along; but, the truth is if you refuse to change, to bend, or be flexible enough to go with the times, then you'll miss out on a lot of what God has to offer in this world. We say God is the same, yesterday, today, and forever; but, the one thing that God constantly gives us is change!

Too many brothers are holding on to yesterday's glory, yesterday's triumphs, yesterday's joy; but, the God I serve has fresh grace and new mercy for us each and every day we live. Somebody said, "great is thy faithfulness, morning by morning, new mercy I see..."

God has so designed the kingdom that it takes diversity to have efficiency. If you know someone who's stuck on yesterday, tell them they need to have a "cup of coffee with the Lord," so they can "wake up" to the new things God is doing in their midst! When all of this Republican backlash is over, the Black Man will be forced to discover no one is going to save him from this mess, but himself! I look forward to the day when we as a race will live up to the standards of love, honesty, faithfulness, kindness, and trust with each other. I look forward to the day when we'll stop living by that tired, worn-out philosophy that causes us to stab each other in the back with our vile acts and deeds:
*We'll learn how to lean on each other more than we do now. It won't be those with the strong muscles who'll carry the day—the days of physical heroes is on the wane.
*We'll have brothers who are strong in love—they will continue to love, even when it's not returned.
*We'll have brothers who are strong in faith—they will live so they

can face their tomorrows with a smile and a ray of hope within them.

*We'll have brothers who'll live a righteous life. Even in the church, too many men are still smoking and drinking—killing themselves and their loved ones, too—thinking that's what real men do.

*We'll have men who will stick with their families, even when the going gets rough, money gets funny, times get hard, and friends are few. The power to change old habits and ways cannot be found in Muscle Magazine! It cannot be found in friends! They have their problems too! Neither your degree nor your pedigree will lead you to this power! If you want this power, you must learn to lean! I heard the song poet say:

> "Learning to lean, learning to lean,
> learning to lean on Jesus;
> finding more power than I've ever seen,
> I'm learning to lean on Jesus."

That's what was disturbing about that first Easter! They went looking for things to be as they were—or as they should have been! They were looking for Jesus to be as they had seen him—dead! Dead, and in the grave! But, God had changed the setting and the scene. Late Saturday night, He unwrapped Jesus' grave clothes, hooked the Holy Ghost up to his heart, and jump-started his spirit. Then he gave Jesus traveling orders to go into hell and preach the first "Emancipation Proclamation Sermon" to those souls in torment. But, early Sunday morning, before:

*Mary could get to the tomb;...

*That old Banty rooster could crow for day...

*The sun could rise from it's bed in the East, and start it's journey to its' Western resting quarters—Jesus, got up from the grave:

*He shook the dust off his dashiki,

*He straightened his dread-locks,

*He dusted off his gabardine slacks, wiped the dirt off of his Johnston & Murphy wingtips, stood on resurrection ground, and declared, "All power in heaven and in earth is given unto me."

That's what disturbed them! They didn't find a dead man, they found him alive! The songwriter said:

> "I serve a risen Savior, He's in the world today.

I know that He is living, no matter what they say.
I see His face of beauty, I hear His voice of cheer;
and just the time I need Him, He's always there.
He lives, He lives; Christ Jesus lives today.
He walks with me, and talks with me,
along life's narrow way.
He lives, He lives, salvation to impart,
you ask me how I know He lives,
He lives within my heart."

One more thing about those disturbed, disgusted, and dejected sisters in that graveyard. They were full of emotions: fear, amazement, astonishment, wonder, awe, and joy! When you and I read this story, however, we do so with a 20th century mind. In retrospect, we think the women should have been doing cartwheels in the graveyard! That they should have been shouting, "hallelujah," giving glory, honor, and praise to Yahweh. But, if you were there on that morning, perhaps the last reaction would have been joy.

Think about it: they were two women going to a tomb where 36 soldiers were stationed. I don't know about you; but, I don't know many women who will go to a graveyard at dawn, by themselves, knowing there are 36 soldiers standing around with nothing to do. It would be hard to feel excitement about anything that came up, even, Good News! It just wasn't the atmosphere and ambiance for that kind of party!

The text says, "while they were on their way, Jesus met them and exclaimed, "all joy!" That teaches me: God has to get us alone, before we can appreciate what He's done for us!

*Adam and Eve were in the garden, alone, when God came walking in the garden, in the cool of the evening, and said, "Adam, where are you?"

*Moses was on the back side of Mt Sinai, alone, when God said, "go down, Moses, and tell Pharoah, let my people go."

*David was on his sick bed, alone, when he realized what God truly meant to him, and said, "The lord is my shepherd, I shall not want..."

*Hezekiah was on his sick bed, alone, when he turned his face to the wall, and the Lord gave him15 more years to live.

*Esther was in the castle, alone, when she had a talk with YAH-

WEH, and got up from her knees, and said, "if I perish, I perish, but, I am going to see the King..."

*Daniel was in the lion's den, alone, when God gave the lion lock-jaw, and made a pillow of the lion's mane, so his servant could sleep.

*Shadrach, Meshach, and somebody said, "A Bad Negro" (Abed-nego) were in the fiery furnace, alone, when God installed an instant air-conditioning system and cooled the furnace which had been heated seven times hotter than usual.

*Jesus was in Gethsemane, alone, when he had a little talk with his Father, saying "if this cup can pass from me?" (Aren't you glad Jesus didn't put a period at the end of that sentence? For if He had, there would not be a Good Friday or an Easter Sunday! I'm so glad He didn't put a period there; but, a conjunction, ("nevertheless!") I am so glad He said, "nevertheless, not my will, but thy will be done."

Beloved, you and I cannot appreciate what God has done for us while we are in the crowd, either! However, when you and I are alone, when we have no one and nowhere else to turn, that's when we really call on God—isn't that right? And I'm not talking about reciting some pious platitudes or some pompous prayers, either... You wait until you get sick, in trouble, the doctor turns her back on you, the family's not around, friends are few, times are tough, and the hills get harder to climb—that's when you will really appreciate who God is, and what God can do!

I may be young, but my theology is old fashioned. I believe for each of us there's coming a day, when we will have to make the last trek to God all by ourselves! You will not come to that moment two-by-two, or three-by-three—no, no! As our elders used to say,

"You've got to walk that lonesome valley,
you've got to walk it for yourself.
Can't nobody walk it for you,
you've got to walk it for yourself."

I don't know how you respond when life upsets your plans, your peace, and your prosperity. But, when it comes to handling what disturbs me and my house:

"I will trust in the Lord,

I will trust in the Lord.
I will trust in the Lord,
I will trust in the Lord,
'till I die."
*I'm gonna trust God for my life!
*I'm gonna trust God for my family!
*I'm gonna trust God for my friendships!
*I'm gonna trust God with my health!
*I'm gonna trust God for my money!
*I'm gonna trust God with my hopes!
*I'm gonna trust God with my children!
*I'm gonna trust God with my tomorrows:
"When you walk through a storm,
hold your head up high,
and don't be afraid of the dark.
At the end of the storm,
there's a golden sky,
and the sweet, gentle voice of the lark.
Walk on, walk on, with hope in your heart,
and you'll never walk alone..."
(Why do you say, "we'll never walk alone, Harlem Park Preacher?)
Because, the songwriter told me:
"He walks with me, He talks with me,
and He tells me I am His own,
and the joy we share as we tarry there, none other has ever
known..."

(THE DOOR OF THE CHURCH IS OPEN!)

"It's A Love-Haunted World"

(This sermon was preached at Unity UMC on October 19, 1997.)

Philippians 1:1-18 (9-11)

Afew weeks ago, I came across a book by this title. I was so intrigued I picked it up, and wound up buying it. Something about the title reminded me of my youthful fascination with horror and mystery books and movies. When I was growing up, my parents wouldn't let me stay up late to watch those films starring Lon Chaney, Boris Karloff, and Bela Lugosi. But, that made me more and more fascinated with such films as "Frankenstein," "Dracula," and "Wolfman." As I got older, I lost my fascination with this type of entertainment. But, every now and then, I will pick up a good mystery novel to read, or sit, watching one of those old horror classics.

My fascination with mysteries is not all that unusual. I imagine some of you have also sat enthralled by one of those captivating tales, or picked up one of those good old mystery novels and read it through without putting it down, too. But, just in case there are some who scowl at this type of literature and genre of film, thinking it is beneath you, there is one such book you have been reading most of your life, and it deals with the same subject matter: mystery and horror. This book is part of a larger book that is still the best-seller of all times. The author used a single name as his "nome de plume," and wrote the whole thing while in a trance on a small island some years ago.

There are only 22 chapters to the whole book. That's right! The title of this book comes from the Greek word, apokalupsis, which means "disclosure of that which was previously hidden or unknown."

Do you give up, yet? Well, the title of this book is "The Revelation," and the author was a brother, named John, who composed his entire works while on the isle of Patmos.

The premise of the book, It's A Love-Haunted World, is: God is present and involved in everything that happens in the world. Like a ghost, He is right in the middle of everything, yet unseen. That's a fascinating thought, isn't it? God is everywhere, all the time, just lurking in the background, only a prayer away. It's as if His love is *haunting* this world.

As we continue the celebration of Pentecost, the season of the Holy Ghost's presence in the world, it makes the title, It's A Love-Haunted World, even more profound. For, isn't that what the word of God teaches? "For God so loved this world..." said John, "he gave us His son...;" and, after Jesus got on board the morning train, he left the Holy Ghost to continue haunting our every move. God seems to be like the words of that popular, secular song of a few years ago: "every breath you take, every step you make, every bond you break, every smile you fake, I'll be watching you."

In our text this morning, Paul seems to use this same idea in his writing to the Philippian Christians. It is conspicuous by the tenderness and care with which he wrote this missive that love is haunting the relationship between he and the brothers and sisters at Philippi. After a brief introduction, his customary word of "thanks" to God for them, and a brief soliloquy about how much he misses the strength this fine group of Christians possesses, he turns to what might be called some doctrinal directives for the brothers and sisters. Listen: "and this I pray that your love may abound yet more and more in knowledge and in all judgment..."

Paul does not merely want their love to grow, but he wants it to become "rich in knowledge and judgment." In other words he does not want them simply to be haunted by love, but to have accurate knowledge of love, and to know how to apply that knowledge to their everyday life. You see the Philippian church was going through some tough times. There were some Jews who had claimed to have converted, but had only changed their head, not their heart.

Along with a group called the Antinomians—who didn't believe that Christ had died a bodily death on the cross—they were wreaking havoc in the church. The Philippian Christians were fighting among themselves. so much so, they were losing their focus on God. In order to encourage them, he wishes they would be haunted even more and more by the love of God.

The same thing is happening in the church today. There are groups of Christians—even here in Unity—who have their focus on everything, but God. They claim to have converted to Jesus Christ, but it was a head—not heart—conversion, too! The evidence: their actions are guided by what they think, not by God.

They want to do anything and everything, instead of working through the Holy Ghost to do what God wills them to do. Anytime people in church are doing "their-thing" instead of God's, there will be trouble in Zion:

*Come here Moses! You had to wander in the desert for 40 years—why? Because the people you were leading were haunted by the memories of the fleshpots of Egypt, instead of the Holy Ghost! They were not impressed by tablets of stone, or God's first "Meal on Wheels Program," or even water from rocks in dry land. Your hardest problem was not getting the Hebrew People out of Egypt, but getting Egypt out of the Hebrew People!

*Come here David! You had been made king of Israel, captain of the Army of the Lord, but what happened? You were on the roof of your castle one day, and you saw a haunting, brown frame. You were smitten—not with the vision of God; but, with your lust for another man's wife!

*Come here Esther! You were trying to live a cool, calm, and copestetic life, until Vashti told the king she was not bowing down before a bunch of drunken men. You were catapulted to the king's harem and became one of his favorites. Just when you thought you had it made, this dude, Haman forced you to expose yourself to being killed for approaching the king's throne without permission! But, you were haunted by your love of your people, so you said, "if I perish, let me perish, but I'm going to see the king."

*Come here Brother Job! You lost everything: your children, your houses, your money, your servants, your stock, even your health. Mrs. Job must have had an insurance policy on you and, undoubtedly, wanted to cash it in. So she told you, "why don't you curse God and die?" But, you weren't haunted by what you had lost—no, no! You were haunted by God's power and ability to do what He wanted. So, you told her, "the Lord giveth, the Lord taketh away, blessed be the name of the Lord!"

That's what Paul was telling the Philippians—and us: no

matter what's going on around you, don't let nothing or no one get your mind off the presence, the power, and the love of God in your life:

*though the devil gets in the choir—don't stop singing for the Lord!

*though the devil gets in the pew—don't stop praising God, because, "when praises go up, blessings (do) come down."

*though the devil will get in your home, keep praising and praying, because "nothing can separate you from the love of God that is in Christ Jesus..."

*though the devil gets in your boss or your coworker—don't let it turn you around. Just keep on saying, "Father, I stretch my hands to thee, no other help I know, If thou withdraw thyself from me, oh, wither could I go."

*though the devil gets in the meeting—keep on being patient and kindhearted. 'Cause the word says, "tribulation worketh patience, and patience bringeth hope, and hope never faileth." Let your hope be "built on nothing less, than Jesus' blood and righteousness," "dare not trust the sweetest frame, but wholly lean on Jesus' name." Whatever they do, you tell them, "on Christ, the solid rock I stand, all other ground is sinking sand."

*though the devil gets in that brother or sister in the church, you keep on haunting them with good, old-fashioned Agape love. Keep on lifting them up in prayer, keep on asking God to change their mind. When folk don't want to listen to the pastor, or don't want to work with the pastor, when there ain't much else I can do to convince them that God wants it done decently and in order, I ask God to either change their mind about me, or change my mind about them. And soon, I discover where there was an enemy, God has placed a friend; where there was strife and friction, God has made a way out of no way! Love makes the difference—every time!

Didn't David say, "Yea, though I walk through the valley of the shadow of death, I will fear no evil, for thou art with me. Thy rod and thy staff comfort me, thou preparest a table before me in the presence of mine enemies; surely goodness and mercy (those twin angels) will follow me all the days of my life."

Didn't David say, "The lord is my life and my salvation,

whom shall I fear? The Lord is the stronghold of my life, of whom shall I be afraid? When my mother and my father forsake me, then the Lord will take me up. I had fainted, lest I believed I could see the goodness of the Lord, here in the land of the living."

As I take my seat, let me reiterate: Paul informs the Phillipian Christians—and us—to remain humble when he says, "that ye may be sincere and without offense..." Then, he tells what this "haunting love" will do for them, and by whom it works. He says, "being filled with the fruits of righteousness, which are by Jesus Christ, unto the praise and glory of God."

He's telling them—and us—everything which comes to us (good or bad) comes through Jesus Christ—it is haunted by the presence of God. God designed it thus, so He could get the praise out of our lives.

He's saying that all of life—from the earliest rocking of our cradle to this appointed time—is understood in the life of Jesus, and he lived his life—as we ought to live ours—so God can get the glory and praise out of it!

*How many of you this morning are spinning your wheels, patting yourselves on the back—like some little Jack Horner—talking about what a good guy or gal am I?

*How many of you devote all your energy to success for yourself, and only give a few, measly moments to the master in prayer and devotions?

*How many of you are having it hard? Children won't act right, job is giving out pink slips, first one tragedy then another strikes. The whole world seems poised on your shoulders, and is turning you every which way, but loose!

*How many times have you asked God to take this burden, or that cross off you, and the more you prayed, the colder God's answer seemed to you?

Well, Brother Paul says the reason God haunts this world with His Love is to help us grow to the place where we give the praise and glory to God—no matter what's going on in our lives— whether we're "on the mountain, where the sun shines so bright, or (whether we're) in the valley in the darkness of night(s)..."

I hear somebody saying, "Listen, Harlem Park Preacher, I don't know about you, but if the truth be told:

90   A Voice In The Wilderness

*it's hard to praise God when there's darkness all around,
*it's hard to praise God when there's sickness and suffering in my midst,
*it's hard to praise God when the evil of the world is in my heart, in my home, in my spirit,
*it's hard to praise God when calamity after calamity strikes like lightning bolts..."

"Do you mean I'm supposed to praise and magnify God when all around my soul is giving way?" That's exactly what Paul teaches us: no matter what happens, whether you're up or down, high or low, winning or losing—keep on trusting in God, keep on praising God, keep on believing in God, and God will see you through!

> Louisa M. Stead, who wrote many great hymns
> of the church, had a great tragedy in her life.
> She had wanted to be a missionary to China,
> but her health prevented her. Then God
> converted her heart one night in Chicago,
> and shortly thereafter, she met William Stead.
> They married, and had a darling, little daughter.
> (As she tells the story) While on the beach
> of Long Island, one hot, summer day,
> she and her family saw a young boy
> struggling in the water some distance from shore.
> While she yelled for help, her husband stripped
> off his clothes, leaped into the water,
> and swam to rescue the boy.   When he reached
> the lad, the boy was so scared he continued
> to fight and kick against his rescuer.
> Mr Stead quickly became tired from trying
> to fight the boy, and the water. Soon,
> they both disappeared beneath the waves.
> Later that day, their bodies washed up on
> shore, and Louisa Stead had to face the
> rearing of her daughter, alone.
> Things continued to get rough, and one day,
> she found herself with nothing to eat,
> no money, and hardly enough heat in the

house to stay warm. So, she and her daughter,
Lilly, sat at the kitchen table, and prayed to God.
In the middle of all that hardship they lifted
up their voices in praise and prayer to God,
and went to sleep.
In the morning, she went to the door,
and there was a large basket of food and supplies
on their porch, and an envelope with money
to buy shoes for her daughter.
That day she sat down and penned
the words to this great hymn of the church:
"Tis so sweet to trust in Jesus,
Just to take Him at His word,
Just to rest upon His promise,
and to know, "thus saith the lord.

I'm so glad I learned to trust Him.
Precious Jesus, Saviour Friend.
And I know that thou art with me,
will be with me 'till the end.

Jesus, Jesus, how I trust Him.
How I proved Him o'er and o'er.
Jesus, Jesus, Precious Jesus,
O, for grace to trust Him more."
That's right—whatever is going on in your life, just keep on prais-
ing the Lord, and see won't this *haunting love* bring you the *fruits
of love*. I hear somebody saying, "I know what the *fruits of the spirit*
are; but what are the *fruits of love?*" (I'm so glad you asked!) The
fruits of love are what you get from having the haunting love of God
in your life:
Joy is *love's* strength.
Peace is *love's* security.
Long-suffering is *love's* patience.
Gentleness is *love's* conduct.
Goodness is *love's* character.
Faith is *love's* confidence.
Meekness is *love's* humility.

and *Temperance* is *love's* victory.

Are you being *haunted* by your past, your mistakes, your loneliness, or by the ways of the world? Let the love of God come into your life. Let God fill you, chill you, thrill you, still you, mold you, make you, stir you and shake you. The song-poet said:

> "The love of God guides me along my way
> The love of God never lets me stray.
> The love of God will always be there, for
> The love of God is everywhere..."

*It *haunts* me when I sleep,
*It *haunts* me when I weep.
*It *haunts* me when I am up,
*It *haunts* me when I'm down.
*It *haunts* me when I'm lost,
*It *haunts* me when I'm found.
*It *haunts* me in the day,
*It *haunts* me in the night.
*It *haunts* me when I'm wrong,
*It *haunts* me when I am right.

I like the way the song-poet said it:

> "He has always been by my side;
> He has always been my guide.
> When my friends walk away,
> And turn their backs on me—He stood right by my side."

(THE DOOR OF THE CHURCH IS OPEN...)

"Can The Black Family Be Saved?"

(This sermon was preached at Unity UMC in February 9, 1998, for Black History Month.)

Matthew 6:9-13

Buried at the heart of the Lord's Prayer is the petition, "Deliver us from evil." Today, evil is all around us. It comes in so many forms, the number and variety defy description. This evil is so vacuous, and manifests itself in various tempting, seductive circumstances and environments.

*Evil comes in the form of a "hurtful heredity" that clings to each new Black generation like a stubborn winter often seems to stifle a struggling spring.

*Evil comes in the form of wayward passions within us, that boil over like an erupting volcano.

*Evil comes in the form of world dangers that overwhelm so many, they lose heart and hope in this weary world.

I am sure you join me, this morning, in reciting that portion of the Lord's Prayer, "Deliver us from evil." And, when we look at the Black family, today, one can say with assurance, evil is undermining it's progress:

*evil is corrupting the minds of our young folk;

*evil is corrupting the school system and causing our children to learn more about dancing, dressing, and dribbling, than reading, writing, and 'rithmetic;

*evil is corrupting the marriage bed and making it a place of whoredom;

*evil is corrupting the business world causing the rich to keep on getting rich, while the poor keep on getting poorer;

*evil has taken hold of our political leaders and made them more concerned about being served than they are about serving others;

*evil is corrupting our churches, causing folk to want things to be done their way in the church! The only place you can have it your way is at Hardee's Restaurant—not the house of God;

*evil is causing the Black family to come apart at the seams.

Children are raising children; the infant mortality rate among us is no better than the rate in many third-world countries; there are more Black men in jail and prison than college; our streets are full of pimps, prostitutes, tricks, and "tricksters;" our children are more concerned about the "Prince of Rock," than the "Prince of Peace," who will be their rock in a weary-land! Yes, evil is all around us!

Whenever this evil stuff starts getting to me, I pick up my weapon, the Bible, and take another look at the wide, panoramic view of where the human spirit began, and just how far—by the Grace of God—the people of God have come in this on-going war. Yes, when I pick up my weapon, I read words, phrases, and passages that accelerate my adrenaline, make my muscles quiver, my tensions subside, and my hopes rise. Because of the lyrical, mystical power of this Book, I am compelled to have a higher view of my circumstances, than I did before. My hope is stirred, my compass is steadied, as I realize that herein is the record of our human encounter with the evil in this world, and how our God made a way for us through this evil—in spite of this evil!

Because the Bible tells me, I am persuaded the Black Family can be saved! Yes, scripture tells me so; but there are some facts and illusions that must be understood about the Black Family before we can understand how! Go with me in imagination to our brief, but brutal history in America.

(I understand our history did not begin in America—it began in Africa! I know our history goes back to the dawn of creation, when scripture says, "darkness covered the face of the deep." But, for our purposes, I want to begin in America, I want to begin in slavery!)

The traditional African's life was patriarchal, polygamous, communal, tribal, and was organized around elaborate kinship ties. There was a strong sense of family and community. Our lives, our identity depended on the tribe, there was no life without it. (Let me disabuse you of the notion that Africa was the utopia some would have us believe. It was not the uncivilized society and culture Hollywood has tricked many into believing it was, either!)

What slavery did was break-up our extended family ties, tear down our sense and reality of community found in tribal life, and alienate us from having an authentic, relationship with our

God, our land, and with each other. Think about it: slavers never picked Africans from the same tribe, so there would be as little communication as possible between slaves.

Originally, males outnumbered females 5 to 1, so slavers would assign numerous men to the same woman for breeding purposes. These two side-effects of slavery—alone—guarantee that little, or no relationships between our ancestors did (or could) occur! So effectively did plantation life destroy the patriarchal life of Africans to many there seems to be no recovery yet!! According to current census update, over 68% of the homes in our community are led by females. Does that sound like our conditions have changed much since slavery?

Many historians and chroniclers of our past have parsed the mistaken argument that religion and the church were—and are—the most important institutions in the Black community. I submit, however, this is a misreading of our brief, but brutal history here. Religion and the church were—and are—important; but, (don't get it twisted!) the extended family was—and is—the most important institution to our survival. The Church is a supportive institution to the family and the community.

This leads to some interesting thoughts when it comes to the question, Can The Black Family Be Saved? (First, I want to tie together my earlier word about the Bible which tells of the deliverance of the people of God, and how that applies to our situation. Is that alright?)

To save the Black Family, we must rid ourselves of the "scapegoat mentality" that's in our minds and our midst. The "scapegoat mentality" is the tendency to blame our situation on somebody else!

In the Old Testament, the Israelites did not atone to God by themselves, saying, "Oh, Lord, where did I sin?" Oh, no! They thought Jehovah was a tribal God, who dealt with them through the tribe, so they held a very interesting ritual, called "The Atonement Ceremony." They would dress a goat by putting cloth around its horns, and symbolically place the sins of the community in that cloth. Then they would lead the animal to the edge of the camp and into the wilderness carrying the sins and evil of the tribe. They called that goat, "the scapegoat." They believed they were absolved of evil and sin by it.

Black people are still "scapegoating" their problems. We want something or someone on whom we can place the blame for the evil amongst us. There are thousands of evils—evils like alcohol & drug-addiction, unemployment, crime and violence, broken homes and marriages, the high drop-out and low completion rates of our students to name a few We still want to throw the blame for them on somebody else—to find a "scapegoat." We need to look in the mirror! When we do, we will see that one of the reasons there is so much evil amongst us is we don't pray!!!

Think about it: our ancestors would begin and end their day with personal and family devotions. They would confront God daily, see His face, and make Him turn His eye on them like a path of sunlight comes across a field at sunrise. In that presence, they would cleanse and renew their spirit. They would say:

"It's me, it's me, it's me, oh, Lord,
standing in the need of prayer..
Not my mother, or my father; but,
it's me, oh, Lord, standing in the
need of prayer."

How do we start our day? By turning on the first news broadcast, or by picking up the newspaper, before we pick up the Word of God. (I hate to tell you; but, there ain't no good news on the news!)

We go to bed, only after we've seen the late news. We spend our days watching the "ignorant box" which produces nothing but images of evil, all day! So, instead of spending personal cleansing time, we join with the public in scapegoating our problems on others.

To save the Black Family, we must go back to the old landmark—prayer! We have to say,

"My faith looks up to Thee,
Thou, Lamb of Calvary;
Be thou, my guide.
Now, hear me while I pray
Take all my sins away,
Oh, let me from this day,
be wholly Thine."

As it was, so it must be! Personal and family prayer will help lift these burdens and boils of evil in our midst. There is no community, family, or home, unless the spirit of prayer is present and practiced by the people living there.

Too many families, under the materialistic mindset of our times, mistakenly view their house as a home. But, what makes a house, a home? Is it the gadgets in the kitchen? The sparkling splendor of the bathroom? Is it the luxury of the living room? The beauty of the bedroom? Is it the custom-hung drapes? The wall-to-wall carpeting? The central air-conditioning? The super-size, color TV? Is it having a freezer full of T-bone steaks? Is that what makes a house, a home? Some Black families mistakenly believe it does!

What makes a house a home is having the love of God, the presence of Jesus Christ, and the joy of the Holy Spirit amongst you. That makes a house a home! You'd best believe if your family does not have all three in the house where you live, all you'll have is:

*custom-draped misery,
*fresh-frozen trouble,
*wall-to-wall confusion,
*televised, color catastrophe,
*and air-conditioned hell!

Finally let me say that: The Black Family will be saved—not by scapegoating; but, by holding on to God's unchanging hand in these changing times!

> I remember one Christmas when my son, Tony
> was about 5-years old, we were going Christmas
> shopping in downtown, Washington, DC.
> As we began our shopping from store to store,
> I admonished him, "son, hold onto my hand,
> so you won't get lost in the crowd."
> After about an hour of shopping, he
> turned to me, and said, "Daddy,
> will you hold onto my hand,
> 'cause I'm too tired to hold onto yours, anymore.

Oops, there it is! That's what the Black Family has to do! We've been holding onto some wrong ideas for more than 400 years; and

we need to let go; and let God!! Black people, whatever it is you've been mistakenly holding onto—if it's standing between you and your God—you need to let it go:
*if it's your money or your pride, let it go...
*if it's your position, or your ambition, let it go...
*if it's your name, your game, or your shame, please let that go...
*if it's that attitude, that's stifling your altitude, you know what to do...
*if it's that matter that's in your mind, then don't mind it, and it won't matter;
I like the way the songwriter put it:
> "Hold to His hand, God's unchanging hand;
> Hold to His hand; God's unchanging hand.
> Build your hopes on things eternal;
> Hold to God's unchanging hand."

(THE DOOR OF THE CHURCH IS OPEN...)

"All That Jazz"

(This homily was preached at St. James Episcopal Church, Baltimore, MD, on February 6, 2000. Father Michael Curry, the rector. The occasion was the annual Jazz Vesper Service, featuring Etta Jones and Houston Person as the musical guests.)

In his book, *The Luminous Darkness*, Dr. Howard Thurman, that great Black spiritualist describes the route a deep sea diver takes as being, "a passage through the belt of fishes." This is a wide band of light, under the water, which emanates from the light above the water. From there (Thurman says) "he moves to a depth of water that cannot be penetrated by surface light. It is dark, foreboding and eerie. The diver's immediate reaction is usually one of sudden fear and sometimes even panic. That soon passes, for as he descends deeper and deeper into the abyss, his eyes slowly pick up the luminous quality of the darkness, and he descends to his destined depth with confidence—using peculiar vision only the darkness provides."

In like manner, when one begins to plumb the depths of Jazz—the only true American art form—one must move beyond the surface of this genre of music, and broach its deep dark depths with no more light than God provides anyone who searches the mysteries of life. And like the deep sea diver looking for buried treasure, the one who searches for the meaning and the message in Jazz must dare go where none else but the spirit can go. For like God and creation, Jazz is a spiritual experience, and what we say God is to religion, Jazz is to music.

Take a journey with me through the hallowed names of this mind-boggling entity we call Jazz. I begin with none other than the inimitable John Coltrane and the beautiful and melodious renditions he recorded of the Broadway tunes, and the sumptuous ballads he delivered on songs like "After The Rain," or "Aiesha." Of course, the sweet sounds of Nancy Wilson, or the stylish scats of the woman Bing Crosby and Frank Sinatra called the greatest, Ella Fitzgerald. Among the hallowed halls of this legacy we find persons like Nina Simone with her super sultry self, or Eric Dolphy who composed so many original tunes as an expatriate from America. Then there's Miles! Yes, miles and miles and more miles of Miles—and those Blue Note boys who accompanied him: Red Garland, Tony Williams and others. The likes of Quentin Warren, Jimmy Smith, King Pleasure, James Moody, Thelonious Monk, Grant Green, "Sassy" Sarah Vaughn, and the vocalizations of "Queen" Dinah Washington.

Nobody did it better than Baltimore's own Billie "Lady day" Holiday, and nobody calypsoed us more than Stan Getz, with "Girl from Ipanema." I recently heard Charles Lloyd on a re-issue of "Memphis Dues Again," that knocked my socks off. Let me hurriedly mention the legacy of my own family tree, the Handy's— from W. C. to John—which populate the halls and walls of our minds and our memories.

There are classic songs like "Moody's Mood for Love" or "St. James Infirmary" (no pun intended, Father Curry) songs recorded and reissued by the likes of Amosos Leontopolus Thomas to Bobby "Blue" Bland. There are the syncopating riffs of big bands like Fletcher Henderson, Chick Webb, and Cabb Calloway, contrasted to the acoustic trio's of a balladeer like Nat King Cole, or the smooth sounds of Jimmy McGriff. Who didn't (or doesn't) have a copy of Dakota Staton (not Station, mind you), singing, "it started at the late, late, late, late show" in their collection. Who doesn't recognize in groups like "Take Six", the origins of close harmony and "scat-like" swing born in the music of Lambert, Hendrix and Ross?

No discussion of Jazz would be right without hearing the name Louis "Satchmo" Armstrong in the verbiage. No library is considered complete without a copy of "Don't Go To Strangers," by our guest musicologists, Etta Jones and Houston Person.

Let me go beyond simply categorizing it's styles and cataloging and chronicling its contributors. As every school boy or girl knows, Jazz is much deeper! Let me get beyond "name calling" or what Howard Thurman described as the level where surface light shines on our inquiry, and plumb the deeper depths of Jazz!

Jazz is worship! It is a prayer from the soul of a people who have longed to be free in substance and style! Just as the

Psalms are Israel's songbook, so the music of Jazz is the effort by Americans of African descent to tell their story and sing their song in a strange land. It is our God-given talent, rehearsed and resourced through the dark nights of the soul, where the whip of slavery was heard, and the suffering and the rape and torture and the mutilation of our people by slave owners and slave traders was felt. That's what Jazz is!

Jazz is the felt and focused fusion of the fact that our families and our folkways were stripped and separated from us, and the sad and criminal reality that we were led along a pathway of pain and pathos until we arrived at a place (for which) James Weldon Johnson said, "our fathers only sighed." Jazz music is our expression of the cruel and callous reality that even after freedom was gained, that same pain and pathos was indelibly stamped in the DNA and genes which comprise (and confound) who we are!!

Jazz is the "strange fruit" immortalized by Billie"Lady Day" Holiday. This fruit grew from the waves of lynching, murder, and oppression started by some hooded cowards, known as the Klu Klux Klan, on Lookout Mountain, Tennessee in 1895. This fruit continues to grow from the current wave of terrorism and violence being perpetrated by contemporary cowards against the Black churches in the South, today!

Jazz is the musical paraclete, that holy sound which accompanied the rise and revival of the artistic and intellectual genius of the likes of James Baldwin, Langston Hughes, Jean Toomer, Paul Lawrence Dunbar, Countee Cullen and Zora Neale Hurston—that group of Harlem, NY "ace-buddies" who put words to the feelings of our people during the Harlem Renaissance of the 1920's.

Jazz is the rhythms, poly-rhythms, and cross-rhythms; the recurring lines and fixed refrains; the spontaneous creations and improvisations; the syncopation and the beat; the antiphonal and pentatonic sounds of the history of our people. This sound was pushed out with all the heart, mind, soul and strength those artists could muster, until that strange sound that no one could define, delineate, or denigrate was heard from the fingers, lips, and vocal chords of a people who had something to say about life and about living.

Somebody said, "the music goes round and round and it

comes out here." We call it Jazz! Yes! This is our story, this is our song! It is just another way of praising our God all the day long!

Yes, Jazz is our people's way of praising God:

*in days when "hope unborn had died;"

*in days when we stood on mountains so bright;

*in days when we walked thru the darkest of nights, where it seemed it was always three o'clock in the morning, and the "sun was never going to shine in our back door again;"

*through days when we worked from "can see to can't see;"

*through days when we had to sing "sometimes I feel like a motherless chil', a long way from home;"

*through days when we marched for what we only felt in our hearts and only heard in our hearing—the strange sound of freedom!

Yes, Jazz is music which documents the reality there's something inside of us so strong:

*dogs couldn't bite out,

*water hoses couldn't wash out,

*Bull Conners and Lester Maddox couldn't beat out,

*cattle prods couldn't shock out; and,

*Jim Crow Laws, Black Codes, and Separate, But Equal couldn't legislate out!

(I hope you're still with me on this flight of consecrated imagination!)

Jazz is the call and response from the depths of a people who because they are "kissed by the sun" suffered the most brutal and dehumanizing form of slavery for over 247 years, saying with every fiber and ounce of being they could muster: "look what the Lord has done in us, through us, and in some cases in spite of us!"

*He took our blue's notes, our field hollers, our chain-gang chants, our "juke-joint jumping" and our slave utterances;

*He even took our spirituals, our songs of faith, and the metered music of Isaac Watts, and those Euro-American hymns we put a beat to;

*He took the music of Wesley, and Sanke, the gospel music of "hard times" and cross-fertilized it with the secular sound of classical notation and swing rhythms and gave us these marvelous, matchless, mysterious, but masterful machinations you and I know as Jazz! Don't think for one moment Christ was engaging in mere Aramaic "chit-chat" when he said, "greater things than these, shall ye do..."!!!

Jazz is our witness to God of the truth of those words. If, by chance, there is somebody under the sound of my voice who says in their heart of hearts, "yeah, Harlem Park Preacher, but I can't understand those strange, improvisational sounds and thrombotic dives into the depths of my psyche as found in some of the musings of folk like Sun Ra, or Archie Shepp, or Pharoh Sanders, or Alice Coltrane's, "Journey into Satchinanda," or Rashan Roland Kirk's, "Bright Moments," or the nonsense notions called "scat" of an Ella Fitzgerald or Sarah Vaughn. Is there anyone who feels that way? If so, take a look at our history.

When brought here as slaves, the plantation owners separated us according to our languages and dialects to prevent us from being able to communicate one with another—so they thought! But, we communicated in the moans, the chants, and the nonsense language of trying to get the message of hope and help to one another! Though they stamped out our lyrics, we improvised and stylized the language of our enslavers to fit our needs.

The same thing is happening in Jazz, today! We're still improvising, we're still taking what the world gives us, and making it suit and serve the pathos and ethos of our ethnicity and culture. Through this idiom and genre of music we call Jazz, we're still turning our stumbling blocks into stepping stones, still turning our dark nights into bright sunrises; still trying to make a hundred, 'cause 99 and ½ just won't do!

Jazz is our performance and our perspective of protest and praise that we believe there's a God somewhere who has heard our cry and pitied every groan!

Jazz music is our attempt to tell the world: we've come too far, bled too much, prayed too hard, died too soon, been fired too fast, been denied for too long, and been loved too little, and we ain't gonna let nobody and nothing stop us from reaching our goal!

And if you cannot hear it in the lyrics of the vocalist—just listen to the melody, the mystery, and the mastery of the music and of the instruments by the musician, because what we think of our

God, what we think of ourselves, and what we think of our fellow human beings is in there shining in All That Jazz!

(GOD BLESS YOU, TODAY...)

"Bustin' Loose"

(This homily was preached at St. James Episcopal Church in Baltimore, MD in February, 2001 for their annual Jazz Vesper Service. Father Michael Curry, the Rector. The musical guests were the Lafayette Gilchrist Trio. The title is borrowed from a group of Secular Prophets, known as Chuck Brown and the Soul Searchers.)

Thomas Kuhn's study entitled, *The Structure of Scientific Revolution*, gives the world an interesting theoretical approach to the question of how and why changes take place in the scientific world.

Though his ideas are about science, I feel they can serve as a foundation for this Vesper Service homily because much of what he says is applicable to all aspects of life and its varied vicissitudes. You see, Kuhn's thesis is that science does not develop in a smooth, continuous fashion—no, no!

Kuhn says: "science and scientists carry out their daily activities only so long as they have a model—a paradigm that holds as relevant their particular view of the universe. Sooner or later, however, as experiments produce new knowledge, there emerges certain crucial findings that disagree with what the old paradigm predicts. And it follows, ipso facto, when enough of these anomalies and analogies have accumulated, they begin to undermine the authority of the old paradigm.

Subsequently, when the new paradigm wins the approval of the practicing scientists, and becomes (as it were) "normal science", then what has taken place is nothing less than a scientific revolution. All this may seem far removed from the world of Jazz; but, the distance, I purport, is more apparent than real.

For the appeal of Kuhn's assessment is universal in its application—even to Jazz. At the risk of being redundant, I reiterate that if you rewind the tape of history, then you'll see Kuhn's theory is accurate about what occurs in science and every other discipline, as well.

For instance, the revolution started in America in the 17th Century—when aggravated and irritated by being taxed without being represented—the colonists threw off the old paradigm, shook the British colonial powers to the core, and declared: "We hold these truths to be self-evident, that all men (White males) are created equal!" The entire world has never been the same since that revolution! (That same group said Black people were only "three-fifths" of a human! Can somebody please tell me what "three-fifths" of a human looks like? Is that a person with a limb missing, or do they have a shortage of toes or fingers?)

Or consider the 1954 Supreme Court decision that revolutionized and revolted against the doctrine of "separate, but equal." With that paradigm shift, a Black preacher from Montgomery, Alabama began a revolutionary march for freedom that is still underway.

Or take the example of that poor, Jewish boy from the ghetto streets of Galilee, who changed the paradigm of the Torah. He stifled the unscientific "preachments" of the religious leaders of his day to such an extent, they said, "we never heard it on this wise, before." In fact, the message of Jesus Christ was so profound and the paradigm shift so prodigious that it even changed the way we reckon and record time—to B. C. and Anno Domini!

And, there is the other "J.C.", John Coltrane (to be exact!), who at the beginning of the 1960's started a paradigm shift, the likes of which Jazz had never seen before. Taking license from such artistic greats as Ornette Coleman, Thelonious Monk, and Miles Davis, and fusing the atonal syncopation and modality of the likes of Eric Dolphy, Coltrane "busted loose" entirely from the paradigm of Bebop into Avante Garde Jazz.

Others took "swing" jazz from its use of the eigth-note to the quarter-note as the basic rhythmic unit. Still others improvised and emphasized on the harmonic, rather than the melodic interpretation of a piece, while others had utilized more complicated chord sequences. All these led the paragons of the 50's out of the "Swing" and into the "Bebop" era.

But, Trane! Trane! Trane!—oh, how this "J.C." brought— and was—as much of a paradigm shift in music as his namesake was to religion. The particularity and peculiarity of this revolution was the "sheets of sound," technique he perfected. As Trane explained in an interview,

"I found that there were a certain number of chord
progressions to play in a given time, and sometimes
what I played didn't work out in eighth, sixteenth,
or triplets. I had to put the notes in uneven groups
like fifths and sevenths in order to get them all in."

If all this seems too complicated for the layman's ear, suffice it to say that Coltrane's "sheets of sound" revolution belongs in the front ranks of contributions to Jazz. I hasten to say that most musicians would be more than content to lay claim to one single innovation in their lifetime. But, not Trane! He is associated with several!

Out of the mold of that paradigm shift came his next and most astounding contribution: the focus on African tones, sounds, harmonies, and rhythms that produced such quintessential compositions as "Africa Brass," "Dahomey Dance," and "Naima," to name a few.

Sometimes the what of a thing may not be as important as the why of it—does that make sense to you? Thus, considering what Coltrane "busted loose" to, might enlighten us to know something about the why of this shift, too! Just look at the environment of Coltrane's time and era and my proposition, here, becomes pristinely clear.

When we look at the Avante Garde revolution, we see that it was nothing more than an appropriate response to the massive social and economic forces impinging on the urban Negro—we weren't "Black" yet! The increased unemployment of unskilled laborers due to jobs leaving the country, and advances in technology, along with the consolidation of African-American determination to remove the chains of second-class citizenship were features of the times. Later, the movement for independence of Africans on the continent, and the growth of explicit Black-nationalist sentiment in America became catalyst to the cauldron of social change brewing in America.

Just as there were external social factors impinging on "Trane" to promote and promulgate this revolutionary genius, there were some internal ones as well. As Frank Kofsky says in his treatise, *Jazz: Black Music, White Business:* "the majority of Jazz musicians were still engaged in what can only be likened to what

Rashan Roland Kirk termed, volunteered slavery:"

During that era, none of the Black musicians were running any of the record companies, booking agencies, radio stations, or music magazines. On this seminal matter rested much of the frustration, exasperation, anger, and alienation they felt and expressed in their music. Ornette Colemen explained in an interview with A. B. Spellman:

> "The problem in this business is you don't own
> your own product.
> If you record, it's the record company that owns it.
> If you play at a club, it's the nightclub owners
> who charge people to listen to you.
> And then, they tell you your music is not "catching on."
> This has been my greatest problem: being shortchanged
> because I am a Negro, not because I can't produce.
> Here I am being used as a Negro who can play Jazz,
> and all the people I recorded for, and worked for,
> act as if they own me and my product!
> They act like I owe them something for letting me
> express myself with my music! The insanity of
> living in America is that: "ownership:" is what it
> is all about! Ownership is the name of the game."

That's why what you are doing and supporting here at St. James's Vesper Service is so critical and important to the future of this idiom of Jazz music. Here artists and artistry can abide in a comfortable and congenial environment, and their "licks" can be heard and had by us without the interloping of the mentality that so permeated the time when "Trane" was trying to "bust loose" from the sophisticated forms of "entertainment slavery" that had him chained and bound." It was a "Giant Step" for all of Jazz! Let me close with this:

*If none of the foregoing explanation suits and serves as a reasonable rationale for the "Giant Steps" Coltrane took in "Bustin' Loose" from the old paradigm, and revolutionizing this idiom we call Jazz a new "Ascension" of cascading auditory ecstasy;

*If my "Impressions" of his life and lifestyle seem "Out of This World," or like "A Journey into Satchdinanda," or "India," or even like, "A Train to Nowhere;"

*If these "Expressions" of mine don't make clear what "Trane" was thinking and feeling as he broke free to the new heights that he took music and the world, maybe Oswald McCall can help. In his prose, "The Hand of God," McCall said, "when one surrenders their inner heart to God," (as J. C. did), then:

> "Be under no illusion, you shall gather to yourself
> the images you love.
> As you go, the shapes, the lights, the shadows
> of the things you have preferred will come to you,
> yes, inveterately, inevitably, as bees to their hive.
> And there in your mind and spirit they will
> leave with you their distilled essence,
> as sweet as honey, or as bitter as gall.
> Cleverness may select skillful words to cast a veil about you,
> and circumspection may never sleep,
> yet you will not be hid! No!
> As year adds to year, that face of yours,
> which once lay smooth in your baby crib;
> like an unwritten page will take to itself lines
> and still more lines, as the parchment of an old
> historian who jealously sets down all the story.
> And there, more deeply than acid etches steel,
> will grow the inscribed narrative of your mental habits,
> the emotions of your heart, your sense of conscience,
> your response to duty, what you think of your God
> and of your fellowman and of yourself—it will all be there!
> For we become like that which we love,
> and the image thereof is written on our brow."

(LOOK AT THAT "TRANE" GO!)

"Dressed For The Occasion"

(This sermon was preached at Unity UMC on September 23, 2001 on the occasion of Homecoming.)

To everyone who has given thought to the matter, it is obvious just how important clothing is. We no longer regard our attire as simply covering, it is our adornment and a means of our self-expression. It cannot be denied from the "swaddling cloth" to the "winding cloth," most of us pay close attention to what we wear. Indeed, this is not a matter to be taken lightly, nor should it be! There is a right and wrong way, a proper and improper way, an ugly and good-looking way to dress. As long as we wish to make a favorable impression, be an ocular-object of pleasure to others, or advance our own cause, we will give attention to our clothing.

In times past, dress has been the reason for a sermon on vanity or indecency, but, not this morning. No, I don't want to talk about style and fashion today—for those are matters about dress that lead to vain behavior. Actually, I wouldn't even allude to the topic if the inspired writer of Colossians had not used it when he penned the passage, "put on, therefore, as the elect of God, holy and beloved..." This figure of speech Paul used is a daily custom to which everyone can relate. But the apparel he had in mind is raiment far more important than suits and dresses, color or fabric. What he refers to is as far above these mundane matters as heaven is above the earth, and eternity above time. Paul had in mind dressing or arraying our immortal souls in garments of spiritual and everlasting quality. For in the final analysis, what really counts is what we are, not how we look!

When we come to the morning of judgment—the critical question will not be, "what did we do with our physical adornment?" It will be, "what have we done with the possibilities and options of dressing our souls?" The song-poet even suggests that, "these robes of flesh we'll drop and rise...". In other words, this earthly stuff won't even be in the equation! So, Paul gives us some sound advice on how we can be "Dressed For The Occasion."

Have you ever looked at the quality of your soul as a means of self-expression? Just as the sun gives light, and fire radiates heat, your spirit, your soul expresses its quality—or lack of it, too!

Either good or evil is in control! And, your character, your conversation, your behavior, even your physical and spiritual dress code will reflect just who is ruling your soul. The outer dress is a mirror of the dress code your soul is living by, and the way you dress up your soul is of utmost importance, because it can never be hidden. The most stylish and fashionable clothes cannot hide the real person that's underneath. You may deceive your brothers and sisters, but "God looketh upon the heart."

The soul is active: it is always moving, never still; always doing, growing, accumulating new attire for itself. The soul needs culture and training in this matter if you are to be what you wish to be—and ought to be! Your soul has infinite possibilities to realize the highest or the basest potential. Jesus set such high spiritual standards for our souls. He said we can "be perfect, just as our heavenly father is perfect." So, there must be no limit to how much beauty we can robe our souls in. What could be some of the fashionable items we would select if we wanted to be "tres chic" or "a la mode." Let's step into Paul's Christian Boutique this morning, and browse through the racks!

You most assuredly want to have on some "bowels of mercy"— that means compassion. No wardrobe would be complete without it, and it comes in all sizes and lengths. In fact, every twice-born, blood bought, child of God has got to have an adequate supply of this item, for it is by compassion that "we bear one another's burdens and so fulfill the law of Jesus Christ." How often would we fall prey to the nakedness and perils of this world, if it weren't for someone sharing our difficulties? When we turn to scripture, we find magnificent passages on the subject of compassion:

*In Deuteronomy, we are told, "open thine hand wide unto thy brother, to the poor and to the needy."

*Proverbs says, "a virtuous woman reacheth her hands to the needy."

*In Micah, we are told our noblest duty is to our fellow brothers and sisters! For Micah 6 says, "and what doth the Lord require of thee, but to do justly, and to love mercy, and to walk humbly before our God."

In ancient Israel, if a man gave less than one-tenth of his means to charity, they said he had an "evil eye." To this day, Jews are noted for their philanthropy. But, when Jesus came, he demanded even more. Every day, Jesus went much further than doing justly and loving mercy and walking humbly with His God. Every day, He was out hunting for people who needed help, and helping them wherever He found them. His example shows there are two kinds of compassion: one, where you accidentally come across a beggar and give them a handout or a meal. The other, you seek out the poor, the needy, the hungry, the lonely, and the lost, and help them out of their pitiful estate. Didn't the songwriter say,

"Tho Satan should buffet, tho trials should come;
let this blest assurance control.
That Christ has regarded my helpless estate,
and has shed his own blood for my soul."

Compassion is actually seeking the lost, and helping them to a better estate —and that kind of compassion was born on Christmas Day.

Next, you've just got to have a nice "shirt of kindness." Are you abrupt, over-bearing, self-centered, and selfish? If that's your situation, beloved, then your soul is inadequately dressed for this world, and the next! Have you ever had an embarrassing moment, and you longed for someone to come to your rescue? Can you remember how it felt when nobody saw or seemed to care? Then a kind person said or did the right thing and comforted you? You may not remember the color of their garments or the cut and style of their tailoring; but, didn't you feel as if they were the most beautiful person in the world?

That's what happened to the woman at the well. She was use to being scorned, and talked about. But, Jesus broke the color and class barriers, and spoke to her as if she were his equal. She couldn't keep that to herself! Scriptures say, "she ran and told everyone, come see a man who told me everything I ever did." What was amazing to the Samaritan woman was not what he said, but the fact that this Jew had broken the barriers of segregation, and had actually been kind to her.

No wardrobe is complete without a nice collection of humility. You need to wear this everyday. In fact, when you see the robe of kindness on a person, you will always detect the under-garment of humility! You see, humility "suits" kindness. It is impossible for an overly proud person to serve someone else with consideration:
*Pride tramples under foot; while humility exalts.
*Pride wounds; humility heals.
*Pride tries to outdo and undo another; humility leads another to a better place in the sun.

Yes, to walk humbly is an attitude, and we know that it's your attitude—not your aptitude that determines your altitude. It's true—if you humble yourself, then God will exalt you. Doesn't the word say, "every valley shall be exalted..."

Of course, no closet is complete without meekness. Sometimes there is an item of clothing in your closet that you may not particularly care for, because of the way you have to care for it. It has to be washed a certain way or at a certain temperature, and you can't overheat it in the dryer, or with the iron. You even dread the thought of sending it to the cleaners. No matter how delicate or difficult to maintain—you dare not discard it for it wears so well with all of your outfits. That's the way meekness is!

Most people don't like meekness, they like to be bold and aggressive—there just seems to be something a little too delicate about meekness for them. Just like a filmy garment gives you the impression of charm, meekness casts about us an indefinable some-thing that warms the heart and soul. The "grabbing" person repels, but they who expect little for themselves attract. We fear arrogant people, we love meek ones. We may take advantage of the meek, but consciously or unconsciously we seek their com-pany. It's a good investment for the smart shopper to go straight for the aisle where meekness is stacked, for our Lord Jesus has promised you a rich return for your investment! Didn't Christ say, "the meek shall inherit the earth?"

Just to be safe, don't overlook longsuffering! Jesus wore it all the time—just like my sainted great-grandmother wore that old raggedy, gray sweater of hers. It was moth-eaten, threadbare, and had so many holes in it, it looked like a slice of swiss-cheese. I remember wanting to hide it so she wouldn't wear it outside to the clothes line or around the house. Longsuffering reminds me of that old sweater she wouldn't throw away. My great-grand-mother gave many bags of clothing to Goodwill Industries. Each time the truck came, I prayed that sweater would be in the bag. But, before I knew it, out it would come, again. I think she loved that old rag for its sentimental value, and could never bring herself to trash it. It seemed to represent dependability to her, and, she wore it proudly—just like we should wear longsuffering.

As a child, my behavior abused the very heart of my parents. But, I remember, too, how patient and kind they were, and how they forgave me of my youthful indiscretions. Just like that sweater my great-grandmother used to wear and would never throw away, parents seem to wear a garment of longsuffering around their hearts, and never tire of wearing it, either! Thank, God!

I've got one more item you just can't overlook, if you want to be properly outfitted, and complete your shopping spree. In the middle of Paul's Boutique there's a sign which says, "above all things, put on love which is the bond of perfectness." Whenever you get dressed-up, it often happens there is a final touch, a final addition that makes everything else go together. Every-thing may be appealing to the eye, the fit is OK, the style is right, but some-thing keeps your forehead furrowed and makes you turn and twist in the mirror to see what's missing.

For instance, a woman may have on a beautiful and artistic gown; but, the lines don't fall correctly and the symmetry is not achieved until a girdle is added. Love is like that girdle! It gathers all the spiritual qualities of the soul together, and makes them a perfect "piece de resistance," a designer's original. Gracefulness, charm, harmony, these come as accessories to your soul's wardrobe when you add love!

The biggest problem in our world today is not the lack of love, it's the lack of the right kind of love! Too many people are caught up in Eros, instead of Agape love. Just listen to the popular music of today: "That's The Way Love Goes," "Can He Love You Like This?", "Love Is A Losing Game." All these songs talk about the pain of love, the shame of love, the agony of love, or the loss of love. Don't get me wrong, there's a reality to that side of love.

The problem is folk don't get to know the good side of love:
*the kind of love that covers a multitude of faults,
*the kind of love that forgives 70 times 7 times—even when it hurts,
*the kind of love that can hold a marriage together,
*the kind of love that will make you love your enemies,
*the kind of love that makes you obey God's word—even when you don't understand all of it.

Didn't Jesus say, "if you love me, then keep my commandments?" Didn't the song-poet say, "they'll know we are Christians by our love"?

When Jesus confronted Peter after the resurrection, he didn't ask Peter for an explanation of his behavior at the trial. He didn't ask for an explanation of why he had gone fishing, He didn't ask for an essay on faith! He said to Peter (three times): "if you love me, then feed my sheep." That's what God is saying to us, today: "if you love me, then feed the hungry, clothe the naked, visit the sick, give sight to the blind, help the lame to walk, forgive your enemies, do good to those who despitefully use you." "Feed my sheep!"

I don't want to leave Brother Paul's Boutique without telling you about the payment plan—that's the best part of this shopping spree. Unlike other stores, in this boutique you don't need any money! They don't take VISA, Master-Card, or American Express, either. You can't put it on lay-away, and there's no installment-payment plan, no high financing, and no need to beg, borrow, or steal to be on the best dressed list of the Lord.

All you have to do is: "let the word of God dwell in you richly in all wisdom, teaching, and admonishing one another in psalms and hymns and spiritual songs, singing with grace in your heart to the Lord." That's the payment plan! I call it the Master's Plan! And, I know it works because:

"Jesus paid it all, all to Him I owe.
Sin had left a crimson stain,
and he washed and made it white as snow."

A lot of people are really label-conscious. If the clothing does not have the right name on it, or in it, they will not wear it. Well, if you want to be outfitted in a label that has stood the test of time, one you can wear when those Jordache, Calvin Klein, or FUBU labels are moth eaten and threadbare; then "put on Christ!"

Do you want to wear a fragrance that has a sweeter scent than Arpage, one that is stronger than Brut, and offers more protection than Sure, that is milder than Dove, and more charming than Chardin? Then, put on the Rose of Sharon! Get adorned with the Lilly of the Valley. Try Jesus!

If you know Him, you should wear His label proudly, display it in all the right places, and brag about the low cost and easy payment plan He offers. When the Word became flesh, Jesus was clothed in righteousness, dressed in majesty, and crowned with the glory of God. Paul says if we keep ourselves outfitted with these garments, we'll wear the crown of eternal life, too.

I like the way Oswald McCall puts this "wearing business" in his prose, "The Hand of God:"

> "Be under no illusion, you shall gather to
> yourself the images you love. As you go,
> the shapes, the lights, the shadows of the things
> you have preferred will come to you, yes,
> inveterately, inevitably as bees to their hive.
> And there in your mind and spirit they will
> leave with you their distilled essence, sweet
> as honey or bitter as gall, and you will grow
> unto their likeness because their nature will be in you.
> As men see the color in the wave so shall men
> see in you the thing you have loved most.
> Out of your eyes will look the spirit you have chosen.
> In your smile and in your frown the years will speak.
> You will not walk nor stand nor sit, nor will your hand
> move, but you will confess the one you serve,
> and upon your forehead will be written his name as
> by a revealing pen. Cleverness may select skillful
> words to cast a veil about you, and circumspection
> may never sleep, yet will you not be hid. No.
> As year adds to year, that face of yours, which once
> like an unwritten page, lay smooth in your baby crib,
> will take to itself lines, and still more lines,
> as the parchment of an old historian who jealously sets

down all the story. And there, more deep than acid etches
steel, will grow the inscribed narrative of your mental
habits, the emotions of your heart, your sense of
conscience, your response to duty, what you think of
your God and of your fellowmen and of yourself.
It will all be there. For men become like that which
they love, and the name thereof is written on their brow."
I admonish you to shop wisely, prudently, and carefully from this
boutique. Put on the "whole armour of God." Wear it proudly,
and I guarantee you'll be Dressed For The Occasion—whatever,
whenever, or where ever it is!

THE DOOR OF THE CHURCH IS OPEN...)

"You Are Always On My Mind"

(This sermon was preached at Unity UMC on December 28, 2006. The title is borrowed from a Secular Prophet named Willie Nelson.)

Matthew 24:19-20

Christ and his 12 disciples arrive at one of the most disturbing moments they must share. For Jesus must turn to the men he loves, and give them some bad news. He had to tell his buddies, his comrades he must leave them. The time has come for Him to say, "goodbye."

The historical record will show Jesus was not the kind of brother who went around breaking folks' hearts. He was a peculiar man, in a peculiar world, where money, power, and material stuff ruled peoples lives—making them indifferent to their neighbor's plight, pathos, and pain. But, that wasn't Jesus:

*He was an honest friend who had never lied to them;

*He was a kind friend—willing to suffer loss so others wouldn't have to;

*He was a decent friend who never stole anything—except when he borrowed an ass that didn't belong to him. He only did it because he knew it would be easier to get forgiveness for using it, then it would've been to get permission to use it!

The disciples knew Him as a patient man even more than Job had been. They knew Him as a quiet man whose speech drew public attention. To them He was a gentle giant, in a world of moral midgets! To these brothers, Jesus was "a brother above buddies!" He was all things to them, and for them! But, now the time had come for Him to say, "adios", "hasta lavista, baby", "sayanora, "goodbye!"

I can imagine as much as Jesus hated to do so, as much as He hated to see the startled looks on their ebony faces, as much as He hated to witness the tears fall from their eyes, Jesus broke the news: my brothers:

"one of these days,
and it won't be long, You're

gonna look for me, and I'll be
gone. I'm goin' to a place,
where I'll have nothing to do;
but, walk around heaven, all day."

This was shocking news! (I can see the color draining from their faces, as his words sink in.) Suddenly, their dreams were dashed to dust, their hearts and hopes became hostages to helplessness. They felt alone and lonely! Their hearts were shattered into a thousand pieces! Like a 12-voice choir singing on key, they cry out, "Master, wherever you're going, we want to go, too!"

In the middle of crying out to Him, Jesus embraces these brothers' emotions by saying:

"let not your heart be troubled, ye believe in God,
believe also in me; in my father's house are many
mansions, if it were not so, I would have told you.
I go to prepare a place for you, that where I am,
there you may be, also." He encourages them
further by saying, "And, lo, I am with you always,
even to the ends of the earth."

In other words, "you are always on my mind!"

Can't you hear the disciples saying to themselves, "Is this all there is to this? Do you mean to tell me after all you taught us, showed us, and did for us... After all the stuff we went through with you—after all this and that—all you have to say to us is, "you are always on my mind?"

*"What good will that do me when my heart's on fire from the pain of life's losses?"

*"What can that do for me, Jesus, when old Satan is on my back, and that brother is hittin' and stickin' like Popeye's chicken!"

*"Why Jesus that seems so insignificant, so minuscule, so putric, so pitiful, and so pale in comparison to the pain, the pathos, the poverty, the persecution, the puzzling places and the problematic people we've got to face."

I can imagine them saying to themselves, if not aloud:
"How does, "you are always on my mind" help me when the going gets tough and the hills get hard to climb?"

*"What will that do for me when my money gets funny and my friends are few?"

120   A Voice In The Wilderness

*"When I've lost my job and my rent is due, and the meal-barrel's empty, and my credit is bad, and my family is sad, and my heart has got more aches than George Bush has ego?"

* "What will 'you are always on my mind' do for me then, Jesus?"

If the truth be told their question is not rhetorical. There are days when the tide goes out, and it seems like it's never coming in again. At those times in your life, didn't you look for something more substantial than hearing some sacred saying, some ecclesiastical epitath, or some pious-platitude, like "you are always on my mind?"

Beloved, on this last Sunday of 2006, and the last Sunday of my 18-years of ministry here, let us take a good, long, hard look through our spiritual-microscopes and see if there are some lessons about life and living in the language of our Lord?

This text teaches me that *"when we are on the mind of Christ, nothing and no one can separate us from Him, or Him from us!"* In the great epistle to the church at Rome, Paul elaborates on this, by saying:

"Who shall separate us from the love of God
that is in Christ Jesus? Shall tribulation, or
distress, or nakedness, or peril or sword? For
I am persuaded that neither death, nor life,
nor angels, nor principalities, nor powers, nor
anything under creation, shall be able to separate
us from the love of God, that is in Christ Jesus,
Our Lord."

It's the same thing—said in a different way—the song-poet was singing, when he harmonized:

"I've seen the lightning flashing, I've heard the
the thunder roar. I've felt sins breakers dashing,
trying to conquer my soul. But, I heard the
voice of my savior, telling me to fight on.
He promised never to leave me, never to leave me
alone. No, never alone. No, never alone.
He promised never to leave me, never to leave me alone."

(Can I deliver you to the scene?) At the very moment Jesus said, "you are always on my mind" to that rag-tag group of his wearied friends, those men faced an uncertain future:

Sermons and Homilies for Urban Ministry   121

*They would live in fear of the very world they lived in!

*They would stand in fear of retribution from the Romans.

*They were to face many afflictions from the Jews.

*They would have to deal with tribulation, humiliation, retaliation, even death at the hands of their enemies.

Simply knowing Jesus was thinking about them made them feel like they "could run through a troop, and jump over a wall." And, (Oh, hallelujah!) after the Day of Pentecost came, and they had received their Baptism of Fire (just like these Watotoes received their Baptism of Water, today) they could say:

*"Come on world—I've got a winner on my side!"

*"Come on woe—You can't make me worry."

*"Come on liars—I've got the whole truth, and nothing but the truth, so help me God."

*"Come on rulers of darkness—I've got the 'bright and morning star' to see me through you."

*"Come on bullies—I've got a born-again body that you can't beat or bother."

*"Come on Devil—what you mean for evil, God will turn to good."

*"Come on..."

I believe in my heart of heart's those brothers could say it because Jesus was their sunshine in the midst of a thunderstorm:

*They could say it because Jesus was their strength for today, and their hope for tomorrow.

*They could say it because Jesus was the healer of their hurts, the balm for their bodies, and the medicine for their minds.

Beloved, when Jesus says, "you are always on my mind," He's not just talking to the disciples of yesterday—no, no! He means everyone in this building, too! So many of you need to hear this "good news" because all you're hearing is "bad news!"

*You hear "bad news" about death and dying;

*You hear "bad news" about sickness and suffering;

*You hear "bad news" about the weather;

*You hear "bad news" about "crime in the streets;" but, not "crime in the suites;"

*You hear "bad news" about war, and rumors of more wars;

*You hear "bad news" about the cost of living going up, while the money needed to live on is going down!

*You hear "bad news" about people losing their jobs, losing their homes, and some even losing their minds because there is so much "bad news," today!

So much "bad news" is causing heart attacks. We need to hear more "good news" because "bad news" is causing families and friends to turn on each other, instead of to each other. This "bad news" is even causing folk in the church to give up their faith in God. It's telling them they can't make it, the odds are against them, and they are fighting a losing battle.

Unity, as I leave these sacred portals to where God will lead me, Jesus Christ is saying to all of us, "you are always on my mind!" That's right, Jesus, the Christ is thinking of you, and of me!

(I hear someone saying in their heart, "how do you know that, Harlem Park, Preacher?") I know because the God I serve is alive! When Jesus appeared to those disciples, he proved—forever and anon—that He is alive! Didn't the song-poet say it?

"I serve a risen savior, He's in the world, today.
I know that He is living, whatever men may say.
I see His hand of beauty, I hear His voice of cheer.
And, just the time I need Him, He's always there.
He lives. He lives. Christ Jesus lives today.
He walks with me, and talks with me, along life's
narrow way. He lives, He lives, salvation to impart.
You ask me, how I know He lives, He lives within
my heart."

As long as my God is alive, then I know I have some "heavenly help for my human hurts." That's right! Because the God I serve is alive, I am persuaded that everything is going to be alright!

A few days before his retirement as the pastor of Mt. Pisgah Baptist Church in Washington, D.C., somebody asked my uncle, Rev. Dr. Lloyd Young: "Dr. Young, you're going on 83 yrs of age; and you started preaching before churches had good salaries, and retirement plans for their pastors, and you probably haven't contributed a lot to Social Security, and you don't have an IRA or stocks and bonds, just how are you going to make it from here on?"

Dr. Young, looked at him, and said,

"I plan for God to yet be alive."

First, since Christ is alive, it proves God can change any situation! You see, if your problem is not greater than the problem God had of raising Jesus Christ from the dead and from the grave, then God has already demonstrated He has enough power to handle your situation. He can change anything! It does not follow, however, that because He doesn't, that He can't! He can, if He chooses!

Second, if God chooses not to change it, He can conquer it! With the resurrection of Jesus Christ from the grave, God demonstrated He had power over all that was in heaven, on earth, and under it. And every twice-born, blood bought, child of God ought to have an innate confidence that God can conquer (or change) anything.

Third, if He chooses not to change or conquer it, then surely, He can control it! The risen Savior is our primae facie evidence that your God and mine is in control of this world. Didn't Jesus say, "all power in heaven and earth is given unto me?"

Then, if God does not change, conquer, or control the situation, He means for us to continue 'till He comes in majesty and glory. Just as Jesus did for His contemporaries, He reassures us, too, that; "you are always on my mind!" We, too, have the "blessed assurance" that, "Lo, I am with you, always, even unto the end of the earth." The same power that visited those brothers in that Upper Room is available to us. (Can I testify?)

Whenever I feel down and out,
I call on Jesus in prayer; and,
this strange power comes over me.
I can't explain it. I don't understand it—
all I know is my friends never made me feel like this.
Family never made me preach like this!
Money never makes me feel this good.
Sometimes, even when I don't feel like preaching
this power comes from somewhere,
and—sooner than at-once—makes me preach.
It's a strange power.
It lets me know when I'm right or wrong,

strengthens me where I am

weak, and builds me up where I am torn down.
Come on, and say it with me: "I don't know what it is—but, I want it!"

This power will tell you Jesus Christ is thinking of you. If you want to stand still and fight for your tomorrows—you'd better get some! If you want to be able to say, "come on suffering, I've got a Savior"—better get you some of this! If you want your courage to bloom like a flower in the deserts of your problems and woes—you need lots of this!

People will wonder "what happened?" when they see you rejoicing in the midst of sadness, sickness, or struggle. They will want to know how you keep on smiling in the midst of all that pain? When you see other folk drinkin' up, shootin' up, snortin up, givin' up, and throwin' up their hands, this Holy Ghost power will keep you hangin' in there! I tell you this stuff works! Beloved, if I were you, I would order up a double-portion, this morning. Then whatever comes your way, you'll be able to say,

"Blessed assurance, Jesus is mine.

Oh, what a foretaste of glory divine.

Heir of salvation, purchase of God,

Born of his spirit, washed in his blood.

This is my story, this is my song.

Praising my Savior, all the day long."
I'll be singing as I go:

"When peace like a river, attendeth my way,

when sorrows like sea-billows roll. What-

ever my lot, Thou hast taught me to say,

it is well. It is well, with my soul.

And, Lord hast the day, when my faith shall be sight.

The clouds be rolled back as a scroll.

The trumpet shall sound, and the Lord shall descend.

Praise the Lord. Praise the Lord, oh my soul.

It is well, (it is well), with my soul (with my soul).

It is well. It is well, with my soul."

(THE DOOR OF THE CHURCH IS OPEN...)

"But, If Not..."

(This sermon was preached at Unity UMC in January, 2006.)

Daniel 3:13

During the Harlem Renaissance, Langston Hughes, the famous Black bard, created a fictional character by the name of Jesse B. Simple. Simple's life was the quintessential depiction of what life is like for many of us, as we begin the year, 2006. In one of his episodes, while recovering from a bout of pneumonia, Simple receives a visit from a friend and begins to discuss his situation:

> Not only am I recovering from pneumonia; but, everything else has happened to me, too! I've been cut, shot, stabbed, run over by a car, and trumped on by a horse; I've been robbed, fooled, deceived, two-timed, double-crossed, dealt seconds, and right near blackmailed —but, I'm still here!"
> "You're a tough man, I said." "I've been fired, laid off, and last week given an indefinite vacation; also Jim Crowed, barred-out, segregated, eliminated, called black, yellow, red, locked-in, locked-out, locked up, and left holding the bag. I've been caught in raids, caught short with my rent, and caught with another man's wife. In my time, I've been caught—but, I'm still here, daddy-o, I'm still here."
> "You have suffered, I said." "Suffered, cried Simple, my momma should'a named me Job, instead of Jesse B Simple. I've been underpaid, underfed, under-nourished, and everything but undertaken. I've been bit by dogs, cats, mice, rats, polecats, parrots, fleas, chiggers, bed bugs, grandaddies, mosquitoes, and a gold-toothed woman."
> "Great day in the morning, I said." That ain't all,

said Simple, "in this life I been abused, confused, misused, accused, false arrested, tried, paroled, black-jacketed, beat, third-degreed, and near about lynched…"

" Anyhow, your health is good up to now, I said."

"Good health, nothing, cried Simple, waving his his hands, screaming, kicking the covers off, and swinging out of bed. "I got everything from flat-feet to a flat-head. Why man, I was born with the measles, since then I done had chickenpox, smallpox, whooping cough, appendicitis, athlete's foot, arthritis, tonsillitis, backache, mumps, and a strain —but, I'm still here, daddy-o, I'm still here."

"Having survived all of that, what are you afraid of, now that you're almost over your pneumonia? I'm afraid, said Simple, "that I might die before my time."

As we reflect on the complexity of last year's carnage, we, too, can say, I'm still here, daddy-o, I'm still here! It has been through many dangers, toils, and snares that we have come to the 2nd Sunday of 2006; and, even if I don't have all those on Simple's list and litany of issues, his words still speak to my soul, when he says, "but, I'm still here, daddy-o, I'm still here!" For despite:

*too much racism,
*too much violence,
*too much poverty,
*too much white and blue-collar crime,
*too much unemployment and under-employment,
*too many teen-aged parents,
*too much drug and alcohol addiction,
*too many crack-addicted babies,
*too much cancer,
*too much high-blood pressure,
*too much illiteracy,
*too many single-parent homes,
*too much child and elderly abuse,
*too many empty pews in our sanctuary; and,
*despite George W., we can still say, "I'm still here, daddy-o, I'm

still here." That brings me to my text!

King Nebuchadnezzar had learned from Daniel and his buddies, Shadrach, Meschach, and A 'Bad' Negro (Abednego), that their God, Yahweh, was something else. You see, when the king had a nightmare, it was Daniel who told him the dream and the dream's meaning. As reward for this keen asset, the king had given these boys some of the highest positions in Babylon.

Well, you and I know that anytime an outsider gets too much attention, some "homeboy" is gonna get jealous; and, sure 'nuff, the snitchers got busy. (Listen how they "butter-up" the king.) "O king, live forever. Thou, o king, hast made a decree that every one that hears the sound of the trumpet, the flute, the harp, the bagpipes, the bells, and the violin, must fall down and worship your golden calf, and if anybody doesn't do it, they'll be burned to a crisp. We just thought you ought to know those foreigners are misbehaving against your decree, o king!"

That put Nebuchadnezzar in an apoplectic fit (you can read Daniel 3:13 when you get home) for it says he was in, " a rage and a fury." (His face became contorted and twisted like a pretzel.) So, he sends for the lads to inquire about their actions. What is absolutely amazing and astounding is what those boys had the unmitigated gall, the hutzpah, the nerve to reply when queried:

> "O, Nebuchadnezzar, we are not careful to answer
> thee in this matter. If it be so, our God, whom we
> serve is able to deliver us from the burning fiery
> furnace, and he will deliver us out of thine hand,
> but, if not, be it known to thee, o king, that we will
> not serve thy gods, nor worship thy golden calf."

I don't know about you; but, I see some lessons for our living in the language of these lads. I don't know about you; but, I hear some helpful hints for getting us through 2006. So, if you don't mind, I'd like to borrow your consecrated imagination and dig a li'l deeper into this ditty—is that alright?

The first thing this text teaches me is: we ought NOT be careful about trusting God! There are some things we must be careful about:

*we ought to be careful of the friends we choose, 'cause association brings on assimilation, and life in the fast lane can lead to some trouble on our trip.

*we ought to be careful what we eat! Somebody said, "you are what you eat." If you keep putting salt, pork, and cholesterol into your bodies, then you should look for your heart to attack you for what you're doing to it!

Yes, there are some things we ought to be careful about; but, these lads teach me, we ought NOT be careful about trusting God. They were positive they could trust the voice within them, instead of listening to the music of the king.

A few weeks ago, I flew to New Orleans to join the refugees and others in Congo Square for a march and rally against the genocidal practices of our government towards the victims of Hurricane Katrina. I was thinking that if I could trust the pilot of that plane—who I didn't know, and had never seen—to get me from Baltimore to New Orleans, then surely I can trust God even more in the year ahead:

*I didn't know whether the pilot was an A or F student in flight school;

*I didn't know if he ever had an accident before;

*I didn't know if he had a bad night, or a fight with his wife...

But, if I could trust that pilot—whom I did not know; then, I don't need to be careful about trusting God because I have an on-going, right-now relationship with God:

*it was God who woke me up this morning;

*it was God who kept my enemies from my door in the last year;

*it was God who made a way where there was no way; in fact, he is "the way, the truth, and the life."

I don't know how you feel about it; but, I'm gonna trust in the Lord until I die!

The other lesson about life and living I find in the language of these lads is: you can't beat Jesus for showing up, just in the nick of time! The text says the king was so bent out of shape by those boys' answer, he ordered the furnace in the torture chamber to be heated up seven-times hotter than usual. Scripture says the flames were so hot they killed the soldiers who put the boys in the furnace.

I imagine the king had gone back to the palace to get a bite to eat; but, every time he took a bite of that ham hock, his conscience would take a bite out of him. (Sometimes when you cannot sleep, it may not be because of what you ate, it just might be what's eating you!) I imagine the king became so frustrated that he threw the food on the floor, and called for his driver to take him back to the torture chamber. As he came nearer the furnace, he heard singing and shouting going on, so he commanded his guards to open the door. When he looked inside, someone had to grab him and hold him up, for inside the fire and flames were the three Hebrew boys dancing, and leaping, and praising God. Scripture says the king looked a little closer and saw a fourth body in the flames walking and leaping and praising God; and, it looked like the Son of Man!

Is there anybody here who doesn't know who was with them in the fire? That's right—it was Jesus:

*Mary's baby;
*the Lilly of the Valley;
*the Bright and Morning Star;
*the fairest of 10,000;
*my company-keeper in the midnight hour;
*my walking cane and leanin' post.
*my all and all.

You can't beat Jesus for showing up, just in the nick of time:

*He showed up at the temple, one day, and the Scribes and Pharisees were so amazed at His speech; they said, "never a man spoke like this before."

*He showed up at a wedding one day and when the wine had run out, He fixed up a new brew which tasted so good and strong that the guest told the host, "you saved the best for last."

*He showed up at Peter's house just as Peter's mother-in-law took a turn for the worse. They found out that sickness and suffering can't stay in the same room where Jesus is!

*He showed up in the middle of a storm one night; and instead of being storm-tossed; Jesus tossed the storm; and, bid it, "peace, be still."

*He showed up at a funeral, one day, and the Widow of Nain turned her graveyard march into a victory march, then turned around and paraded back to town.

*He showed up at Calvary, one day, when a thief was just about to breathe his last, and told him, "this day, thou wilt be with me in paradise."

But, do I have to go back there for evidence of the power of His presence? Can't somebody here stand up and say, "He woke me up this morning," He put my feet on a street called straight." As I take my seat, be advised, that's the exact kind of faith I am taking with me into 2006—a "but, if not" kind of faith:

*I know He'll show up for me in the New Year; but, if not...
*I know He can make my enemies my footstool; but, if not...
*I know He can move the mountains in my way; but, if not...
*I know He can get the hellions out of the church; but, if not...
*I know He can straighten out my children; but, if not...
*I know He can make a way, where there is no way; but, if not; I'm gonna say, "Halleluiah, anyhow!"

I'll be singing as I go:

"I don't know about tomorrow, I just live
from day to day. I don't borrow from it's
sunshine, for its skies might turn to gray.
Many things about tomorrow, I don't seem
to understand; but, I know who holds
tomorrow, and I know who holds my hand."

(THE DOOR OF THE CHURCH IS OPEN...)

"Eulogy For Kimcina Carey"

(This sermon was preached at Unity UMC on August 20, 2011)

Matthew 22:36-40

There are many codes of living extant and operative in our world today. Some live by the philosophy, "do unto others, before, they do unto you." This ethic stems from the experiences of those who have been dealt a hand from the bottom of the deck of life, and their goal—at all cost—is to get at least one card from the top.

Others live by the code, "I've got mine—you've got yours to get." This thinking suggests the person has been blessed by God; but, are determined not to squander them on those unworthy folk—who just will not pull themselves up by their own "bootstraps." They never consider that many of the needy don't have anything on their feet!

Still others believe they are special, and others should do for them, instead of them doing for others. You know some prima donna's like that—don't you? Doesn't your stomach turn when you realize they are your family, your friends. Growing up, we used to describe them as folk who would drown when it rains, because their noses are stuck so far up in the air.

Then there are people like Kim:

*the kind of person who didn't have a selfish bone in her body.

*the kind of person who would go the "2nd-mile" for others—or at the least, get out of the way!

*a kindhearted, loving mother, a strong supporter of her extended family, an educator, a gentle, sweet-spirited sister, who didn't have an enemy in the world—except that dreaded cancer which finally claimed her tired and ravaged body.

But, today, today:

*we have come to celebrate Kim's life—not her death or her dying.

*we have come to celebrate Kim's life—and the joy that comes in knowing exactly where Kim will be from this day forward.

*we have come to celebrate Kim's life—and to memorialize a young woman who may have left us too soon; but, who will forever be a precious memory in our hearts, minds, and souls.

*we have come to celebrate Kim's life—and to comfort and console her grieving children and loved ones, especially those for whom the perennial question "why" echoes in their hearts like a haunting refrain.

To those who have a heavy heart, whose head is bowed, and whose eyes are wet with tears of sorrow, we say:

*"earth has no sorrow, that heaven cannot heal;"

*"cast your care upon Him, for He cares for you;"

*"my God will supply all of your needs, according to His riches in glory."

If Kim's demise has you frought with feelings you can't explain, or thoughts you can't put into words, I encourage you:

*Look up!

*Look up—God's answer will be found high upon a hill.

*Look up—If Kim's death has you undone, don't look around, don't look down, don't look askance, and don't look back—look up!

*Look up—you'll see that God's heavenly handkerchief is hanging over your head; He promised to wipe all tears from your eyes.

*Look up—that's where Kim is! This is just her frame lying before us. The essence of Kim (her soul) is somewhere on high today.

*Look up—Christ is telling you that death is not the end.

*Look up—Our God wants you to know beyond this veil of tears and sorrow, beyond this evil world of cancer, death, and dying—there's a better place. There's a place where wickedness ceases from troubling us, and weary souls, like Kim's, find peace, rest and comfort.

*Look up—perhaps, you'll hear Kim singing, this morning:

> "When life's transient dream, when death's cold
> sullen stream, shall o'er me roll,
> Blest Savior then in love, fear and distrust
> remove; O bear me safe above, a ransomed soul."

I hope each of us who loved Kim will strive harder to make her dying a reason to take up where she left off—by becoming more selfless, instead of selfish; and,

> "So live that when thy summons comes to join
> that innumerable caravan, which moves to that

mysterious realm, where each shall take its chamber in the silent halls of death; thou go not like some quarry slave, at night, scourged to his dungeon, but sustained and soothed by an unfaltering trust, approach thy grave like one who wraps the drapery of thy couch about them, and lie down to pleasant dreams..."

Finally, on tomorrow, the world will be viewing and cele-brating the unveiling of the Martin Luther King, Jr. Memorial, in my hometown, Washington, DC. What a fitting climax the memorial will be to the dynamic life of this great Black man. It will signify to all that a significant life has passed this way, and this marks the time when it stopped.

May I suggest in addition to the physical memorial Kim's family is going to lay for her at Arbutus Cemetery, you and I—who loved her—become a living memorial for her. "How do you do that, Harlem Park, Preacher?" (I'm so glad you asked!):
*whenever you see injustice—stand up!
*whenever something needs saying—speak up!
*whenever you make an appointment—show up!
*if you're blind to your own faults—wake up!
*if you make a mistake—fess up!
*if you overstep your boundary—back up!
*if you get behind—catch up!
*if they knock you down—get up!
*if you're out of line—straighten up!
*when the elders speak—listen up!
*when the preacher preaches—wake up, everybody!
*when the teacher teaches—sit up!
*when the fight is over—make up!
*if you're being too hard—ease up!
*if your mind is closed—open up!
*if you make a mess—clean it up!
*if you drop trash—pick it up!
*if someone is waiting for you to cross the street—step it up!
*you don't have an entitlement to anything, so—shut up!
*if your brother or sister falls down—help them up!
*if you want to know something—look it up!

*if your pants are sagging—pull them up!
*if your belt is loose—tighten it up!
*if your fly is down—zip it up!
*if the music is wholesome—turn it up!
*if life is good—soak it up!
*if lfe is boring—shake it up!
*if life is unfair—suck it up!
*if life is funny—laugh it up!
*if life is sad—look straight up!
*because life is too short—live it up; and,
*if you're a Child of God—like Kim—then stand up; and say;

> "Am I a soldier of the cross,
> a follower of the Lamb?
> And shall I fear to own his cause
> or blush to speak his name.
> Must I be carried to the skies,
> on flowery beds of ease;
> While others fight to win the prize,
> And sail through bloody seas.
> No! I must fight, if I would reign,
> Increase my courage, Lord,
> I'll bear the cross, endure the pain,
> Supported by thy word..."

Can't you hear her singing:

> "When peace like a river, attendeth my way,
> When sorrows like sea-billows roll.
> Whatever my lot, thou hast taught me to say,
> It is well, it is well with my soul.
> Though satan should buffet,
> though (Cancer) should come,
> Let this blessed assurance control,
> That Christ has regarded my helpless estate,
> And has shed His own blood for my soul.
> It is well! It is well! It is well with my soul..."

(GOD BLESS YOU, TODAY!)

Endnotes

Introduction

    1 B: Evans Crawford, <u>The Hum: Call And Response In African-American Preaching</u>, (Washington, D.C.: Howard University Press, 1995) 13.

    2 B: Martin Luther King, Jr. <u>Where Do We Go From Here: Chaos or Community?</u> 3rd ed. (New York: Harper and Row), 2010) 159.

    3 A: "The City That Bleeds," <u>The Baltimore Sun</u> 12 July 1989: 1.

    4 B: <u>1990 Census Report: Annual Update</u> (Washington, D. C.: U. S. Government Printing Office, 1991) 257.

1. *When Are You Coming Home?*
   1 Ezra 1:3.
   2 Nehemiah 2:6.
   3 Revelation 6:10.
   4 S: "I Got A New Home Over In Glory," author unknown.

2. *Wake Up, Everybody*
   1 John 3:16.
   2 S: Isaac Watts, Lowell Mason, "Joy To The World," 1939.
   3 Luke 2:49.
   4 John 1:36.
   5 Matthew 4:17.
   6 S: Thomas Andrew Dorsey, "Precious Lord, Take My Hand," 1938.
   7 HBCU—Historic Black College/University
   8 S: Ludie Day Pickett, "No, Never Alone," 1897.
   9 S: George A. Young, "God Leads Us Along," 1903.

3. *Get Your But Out Of The Way*
   1 African Proverb.
   2 P: Dr. Miles Jones, "Verse 1," Sermon preached at Metropolitan Baptist Church, Washington, D. C., February 12, 1990.

3 S: W. B. Stevens, "Farther Along," 1911.

4. *Anatomy Of A Bestseller*
   1 P: John Donne, "No Man Is An Island," 1623.
   2 S: "Without God," author unknown.
   3 Psalm 111:10.
   4 B: A. Leon Higginbotham, In The Matter Of Color, (New York, Hougflin-Mifflin Co., 1978) 214.
   5 Galatians 6:7.
   6 Hebrews 12:1.
   7 John 14:1.
   8 S: Thomas Shepherd, "Must Jesus Bear The Cross Alone?", 1693.
   9 Matthew 27:54.
   10 S: Isaac Watts, "Alas, And Did My Savior Bleed?", 1707.
   11 Revelation 1:9.
   12 S: R. H. Cornelius, "Oh, I Want To See Him," 1916.

5. *God-Filled Women In This Godless Age*
   1 William Shakespeare, Hamlet, The Complete Works of William Shakespeare, ed. G. L. Ketteredge (Boston: Houghton-Mifflin, 1936) 1203.
   2 S: "Sometimes I Feel Like A Motherless Chil'," African-American spiritual.
   3 Mark 14:7.
   4 Ruth 1:16.
   5 1 Corinthians 13.
   6 S: "The Love of God," Soul-Stirrers, performers.
   7 S: Dorsey, "The Lord Will Make A Way, Somehow," 1943.

6. *Let's Go Get Stoned*
   1 A: Walter Littlefield, "The Prospects Are Dim," Newsweek Magazine 10 May 1992: 11.
   2 A: "The Los Angeles Riots," The Marin Institute Report 14 April 1992: 2-16.
   3 2 Samuel 22:30.
   4 Matthew 11:28.

5 S: Charles Wesley, "O For A Thousand Tongues To Sing,"
1739.

6 2 Corinthians 11:30.

7 S: "When I Think Of The Goodness of Jesus,"
author unknown.

8 S: James Rowe, "Love Lifted Me," 1912.

9 S: C. Austin Miles, "In The Garden," 1913.

10 S: "This Joy I Have, The World Didn't Give It To Me,"
African-American spiritual.

7. *Back To The Future*

1 B: 1990 Census Report: Annual Update, (Washington,
D. C., U. S. Government Printing Office, 1993) 126.

2 Exodus 13:20-22.

3 Daniel 5:25.

4 I Kings 18:20-46.

5 Luke 9:12-17.

6 Matthew 28:18.

7 Acts 15:25.

8 "Sankofa"—Reaching back to retrieve the best from the
past, while moving forward.

9 S: Isaac Watts, "Come Holy Spirit, Heavenly Dove," 1707.

10 S: Dowel Iverson, "Spirit of The Living God," 1926.

11 S: Magnolia Lewis-Butts, "Let It Breathe On Me," 1942.

12 S: "I Moved From My Old House," author unknown.

8. *You Are Hereby Summoned To Be A Witness*

1 B: Howard Thurman, Deep River and The Negro Spiritual
Speaks of Life and Death, (Boston, Friends United Press,
1975) iv.

2 Matthew 28:18ff.

3 Romans 7:21-24.

4 2 Corinthians 5:17.

5 Phillipians 4:8ff.

6 Matthew 23:15.

7 John 3:2.

8 I Corinthians 13:ff.

9 B: Bob Hope, The Times of My Life, (New York, Knopf, 1993) 23.

10 Matthew 28:18.

11 S: Miles, "In The Garden."

12 S: Watts, "Alas, And Did My Savior Bleed."

13 S: Dorsey, "Precious Lord, Take My Hand."

14 S: Thomas Moore, "Come Ye Disconsolate," 1816.

9. 5 *Smooth Stones*

1 B: David Smalls, The Inner Ear, (New York, McMillan Co., 1982) 8.

2 1 Samuel 17:26.

3 Quote: "Everyone can get in, where they can fit in; and fit in where they can get in," Daren Muhammed, "The State Of The City Radio Show," April 10, 1993.

4 I John 3:17.

5 B: Dr. Martin Luther King, Jr., Stride Towards Freedom, (New York, Harper Press, 1958) 17.

6 S: Civilla D. Martin, "God Will Take Care of You," 1904.

7 S: Edward Moore, "My Hope Is Built On Nothing Less," 1834.

8 S: "The Love of God," Soul-Stirrers performers.

9 S: Cleavant Derricks, "Just A Little Talk With Jesus," 1941.

10 S: Augustus Toplady, "Rock of Ages," 1776.

11 S: Kenneth Morris, "Christ Is All," 1997.

12 S: Andre Crouch, "Oh, It Is Jesus," 1977.

13 S: Will L. Thompson, "Jesus Is All The World To Me," 1904.

14 S: Johnson Oatman, "No Not One," 1895.

10. *A Disturbing Dilemma*

1 B: Jawanzaa Konjufu, Adam, Where Are You?", (Chicago, African-American Images, 1997) 16.

2 Luke 24:6.

3 S: Thomas O. Chisholm, "Great Is Thy Faithfulness," 1923.

4 S: John Stallings, "Learning To Lean," 1980.

5 S: A. H. Ackley, "I Serve A Risen Savior," 1933.

6 Genesis 3:9.

7 Exodus 7:26.

8 Psalm 23.

9 Esther 4:6.

10 Matthew 26:39.

11 Matthew 26:40.

12 S: "That Lonesome Valley," African-American spiritual.

13 S: "I Will Trust In The Lord," African-American spiritual.

14 S: Richard Rodgers and Oscar Hammerstein, "You'll Never Walk Alone," 1945.

15 S: Miles, "In The Garden."

11. *It's A Love Haunted World*

1 John 3:16.

2 S: "I'll Be Watching You," The Police, performers.

3 "Antinomians"—Christians who believed there was no physical resurrection of Jesus.

4 Esther 4:6.

5 Job 2:9.

6 Job 2:10.

7 S: "The Wise Man Built His House Upon The Rock," children's song.

8 Romans 3:9.

9 S: Charles Wesley, "Father I Stretch My Hands To Thee," 1741.

10 James 1:1-3.

11 S: Edward Mote, "My Hope Is Built On Nothing Less," 1834.

12 Psalm 23.

13 Psalm 27.

14 S: Young, "God Leads Us Along."

15 B: Robert Erickson, The African Missionary: The Biography of Louisa M. R. Stead (New York, Wodehose Press, 1948) 117.

16 S: Louisa M. R. Stead, "'Tis So Sweet To Trust In Jesus," 1882.

17 S: "The Love of God," Soul-Stirrers performers.

18 S: "He Has Always Stood By My Side,"
African-American spiritual.

12. *Can The Black Family Be Saved?*
1 Matthew 6:9-13.
2 "   " ' "   ".
3 A: "The Prison Pipeline," Baltimore Sun Newspaper
12 December 1997: 1, 16.
4 B: 1990 Census Report: Annual Update, (Washington,
D. C.: U. S. Government Printing Office, 1998) 118-126.
5 Leviticus 16:10.
6 S: "Standing In The Need of Prayer,"
African-American spiritual.
7 S: Ray Palmer, "My Faith Looks Up To Thee," 1830.

13. *All That Jazz*
1 B: Howard Thurman, The Luminous Darkness
(Philadelphia, Friends United Press, 1989) 2.
2 "Paracletes"—The Holy Spirit.
3 Charles Wesley, Edward Sanke.
4 John 1:50.

14. *Bustin' Loose*
1 B: Thomas Kuhn, The Structure of The Scientific
Revolution, (Chicago, University of Chicago Press, 1962) 3.
2 U. S. Declaration of Independence, paragraph 2, 1776.
3 John 7:46.
4 "Avante Garde Jazz"—Free stream of consciousness-style
of playing jazz music.
5 A: A. B. Spelman, "Interview of John Coltrane,"
Downbeat Magazine 10 August, 1962: 2, 21-39.
6 "Sheets of Sound"—Loosening of the strict chords,
modes and harmonies of hard bop jazz music.
7 B: Frank Kofsky, Jazz: Black Music, White Business,
(New York, Pathfinder Press, 1998) 116.
8 A: Spelman, "Interview of Ornette Coleman,"
Downbeat Magazine 2 October, 1968: 17-22.
9 P: McCall, "The Hand of God."

15. *Dressed For The Occasion*
   1 S: W. W. Welford, "Sweet Hour of Prayer," 1845.
   2 1 Samuel 16:7.
   3 Matthew 5:48.
   4 Galatians 6:2.
   5 Deuteronomy 15:11.
   6 Proverbs 31:10.
   7 Micah 6:8.
   8 S: Horatio Gates Spafford, "It Is Well With My Soul," 1873.
   9 John 4:29.
   10 Isaiah 40:4.
   11 Matthew 5:5.
   12 Colossians 3:14.
   13 S: "That's The Way Love Goes," Janet Jackson, performer.
   14 S: "Can He Love You Like This?", After Seven, performers.
   15 S: "Love Is A Losing Game," Lou Rawls, performer.
   16 John 21:17.
   17 S: Peter Scholtes, "They'll Know We Are Christians By Our Love," 1966.
   18 John 14:15.
   19 Colossians 3:16.
   20 S: Elvina M. Hall, "Jesus Paid It All," 1865.
   21 P: McCall, "The Hand Of God."

16. *You Were Always On My Mind*
   1 S: "Walk Around Heaven All Day," African-American spiritual.
   2 John 14:1-14.
   3 Romans 8:35.
   4 S: Pickett, "Never Alone."
   5 S: Miles, "In The Garden."

17. *But, If Not*
   1 B: Langston Hughes, The Best Of Simple, (New York, Noonday Press, 1961) 245.
   2 Daniel 3:13.
   3 Daniel 3:19.

4 Daniel 3:22.

5 S: "I Will Trust In The Lord," African-American spiritual.

6 John 7:46.

7 John 2:10.

8 Luke 4:38-39.

9 Mark 4:39.

10 Luke 7:12-14.

11 Luke 23:43.

12 S: Ira F. Stangill, "I Don't Know About Tomorrow," 1950.

18. *Eulogy For Kimcina Carey*

1 Luke 6:31.

2 S: Palmer, "My Faith Looks Up To Thee."

3 1 Peter 5:7.

4 Phillipians 4:17.

5 Revelation 21:4.

6 S: Palmer, "My Faith Looks Up To Thee."

7 P: McCall, "The Hand Of God."

8 S: Watts, "Am I A Soldier Of The Cross?"

_____

_____

Legend:

All scripture references are from the Authorized King James Version of the Bible.

A—article

B—book

P—poem

S—song

Epilogue

Asante Sana to my friends, Bishop Carolyn Guidry, and the Honorable Bishop C. Anthony Muse for graciously sharing their gifts and talents with this project. A special *asante* to a special friend, Dwight "Twin" Donaldson for his unwavering support and encouragement.

Be it hereby known that Baba Charles Lowder, graphic designer; and Brother Paul Coates and the miracle working staff of Black Classic Press have done it, again. It is with the substantial work, words, and prayers from all of these that *my* dream can be viewed through the light from these pages.

Ashai, Alleluia, Amen!

The Honorable Reverend Doctor Kwame O. Abayomi

www.ingramcontent.com/pod-product-compliance
Lightning Source LLC
Chambersburg PA
CBHW051208120626
46547CB00013B/1257